LIFE

POPE FRANCIS
with Fabio Marchese Ragona

Translated from the Italian
by Aubrey Botsford

LIFE
My Story Through History

HarperOne
An Imprint of HarperCollinsPublishers

First published in 2024 in Italian under the title *Life: La mia storia nella Storia* by Papa Francesco Bergoglio with Fabio Marchese Ragona. Published by arrangement with Delia Agenzia Letteraria.

FIRST HARPERONE HARDCOVER PUBLISHED 2024

Designed by Netphilo Publishing, Milan, Italy

Library of Congress Cataloging-in-Publication Data has been applied for.

ISBN 978-0-06-338752-2
ISBN 978-0-06-339753-8 (ANZ)

24 25 26 27 28 LBC 5 4 3 2 1

CONTENTS

INTRODUCTION

Let us learn from history, particularly the darkest pages of history, so as not to repeat the mistakes of the past: Pope Francis has made this appeal several times in recent years, underlining the high value accorded to memory in every person's life, a framework that is priceless. We must learn history by studying it in books, of course, but also by listening to the voices of people who have lived through moments that were, for better or worse, unforgettable; of people who have lived a long life; of people who have encountered the Lord on many occasions in their lives and can bear witness at firsthand to what they saw.

In the book of Exodus, chapter 10, verse 2, God tells Moses to show Pharaoh some signs of his power, "that you may tell in the hearing of your son and of your son's son how I have made sport of the Egyptians and what signs I have done among them; that you may know that I am the LORD." The purpose is certainly to surprise and persuade the king of Egypt, but also to nurture his people's memory by passing on his knowledge of God, which believers communicate by telling the story of their own lives.

Those who tell a story will thus render a service to those who are hungry to learn, and offer a warning, particularly to the youngest among us, about what might await them on their journey, describing what has been so as to better understand what will be.

It is no coincidence that, in his message for World Communications Day 2020, Pope Francis declared that humans are storytelling beings, that "from childhood we hunger for stories just as we hunger for food. Stories influence our lives, whether in the form of fairy tales, novels, films, songs, news, even if we do not always realize it."

The book you are holding in your hands is thus born with the aim of narrating history through one person's story: the most significant events of the twentieth century and the first decades of the twenty-first in the voice of a special witness, Pope Francis, who has very willingly agreed to look back on his own life through the events that have left a mark on all humanity.

Life came to light after a series of conversations between the pontiff, to whom I offer enormous and heartfelt gratitude for the trust he has once again placed in me, and the present author, conversations in which Francis opened the door to his heart and memories to send out powerful messages on fundamental topics like faith, family, poverty, interfaith dialogue, sports, scientific progress, peace, and many others. From the outbreak of World War II in 1939, when the future pontiff was not quite three years old, to today, Jorge Mario Bergoglio takes his readers by the hand and, with his memories, leads them on a remarkable journey through the decades, looking back on the most significant milestones of our times. Where was the young Jorge in 1969, as the world watched the moon landings on television? What was Cardinal

Bergoglio doing on September 11, 2001, when the United States was being attacked by terrorists?

Recollections of a priest talking about the horrific extermination of the Jews by the Nazis, the atom bombs dropped on Hiroshima and Nagasaki, Jorge Rafael Videla's coup in Argentina, the fall of the Berlin Wall, the great recession, the resignation of Pope Benedict XVI—events that are intertwined with the life of this papa callejero, this pope of the streets, who gives a rare glimpse into the treasure chest of his memories, with the plain speaking that is so characteristic of the man, to talk about the moments that have changed the world and also his own life.

The pontiff's own voice, in his memories, alternates in each chapter with that of a narrator, who reconstructs selected moments in the everyday life of the future Pope Francis, adding a few details suggestive of the period to set the historical scene and put the latter's words into context.

"Our life is the most precious 'book' we have been given," the pontiff said during a cycle of catechesis he launched in 2022, dedicated to the theme of discernment, "a book that, unfortunately, many people do not read, or rather they do so too late, before dying. And yet, precisely in that book, one finds what one pointlessly seeks elsewhere. . . . We might ask ourselves: Have I ever recounted my life to anyone? It is one of the most beautiful and intimate forms of communication, recounting one's own life. It allows us to discover hitherto unknown things, small and simple, but, as the gospel says, it is precisely from the little things that the great things are born."

And so, turning afresh the pages of the precious book that is life,

Pope Francis will lead us down a road paved with emotion, joy, and suffering, a look through a window on the past that will help us to better know our present—right up to the last chapter, with a history that remains to be written.

—Fabio Marchese Ragona

I

THE OUTBREAK
OF WORLD WAR II

Like every morning, the news is playing on the radio. Mario Bergoglio usually switches it on while he makes coffee in the small kitchen before going to work. The floor is still wet in places: his wife, Regina, has already taken advantage of a brief moment of calm to run the mop over it. The scent and flavor of the steaming, dark beverage remind Mario of Italy and his childhood in the Piedmontese town of Portacomaro, near Asti, like Marcel Proust in Swann's Way dipping his madeleine in a cup of tea and remembering his childhood with his aunt Léonie. Mario's private moment of recollection is interrupted, however, by the crying of little Oscar, his second child, who is giving the neighborhood no peace.

The seven o'clock bulletin, playing in the background, has mostly political news: President Roberto Ortiz has issued a new statement on the Special Commission of Inquiry on Anti-Argentine Activities, set up at the time with the aim of "de-Nazifying" the nation; further disturbances, organized by the General Confederation of Labor, are expected from the workers' movement. In September 1939, Argentina's urban centers are alive with conflicting currents of opinion: the Third Reich has managed to infiltrate a few fringe elements of society, and broadcasts praising the greatness of Germany under Adolf Hitler occasionally make their way onto some of the radio stations.

Having swiftly drunk his coffee, and before leaving the small, brightly colored family home at 531 Via Membrillar, in the Flores district of Buenos Aires, Mario kisses Regina goodbye. She has picked up the toddler, one year and eight months old, to calm him down. The young couple's other child, Jorge, not quite three years old, is ready to leave the house: Rosa, Mario's mother, who lives nearby, will arrive in a few minutes to take him home with her for the day. A ritual that is repeated nearly every day, this is a way for Grandma Rosa to help and support her daughter-in-law as she deals with a thousand domestic worries and, above all, takes care of Oscar.

Mario, after giving his children a kiss too, is standing by the door with his wife when, in a rare moment of silence, they are suddenly aware of a particular item on the radio, among all the other pieces of news from abroad: Neville Chamberlain, the British prime minister, has announced that his country is at war with Nazi Germany. The ultimatum he presented a few hours earlier, in response to the invasion and bombing of Poland, has been left unanswered.

It is the beginning of the Second World War, but this is not immediately understood, particularly in South America. It is a news item like others in Argentina, close to the end of the broadcast, just before the musical interlude, but this Italo-Argentine couple is shocked. Their thoughts fly first to their cousins and other relatives living in Europe, as they are assailed by memories of the horrifying stories of the First

World War they have heard a thousand times from Mario's father, Giovanni, who fought at the front. But their feelings of sadness and worry disappear a few seconds later with two firm raps on the door: Grandma Rosa has arrived, and the sudden commotion finally silences Oscar, to everyone's relief. Jorge, seeing his grandmother come in, runs into her arms.

What a wonderful woman! I loved her so much. Grandma Rosa, my paternal grandmother, was a key figure in my growth and development. She lived no more than one hundred fifty feet from our home. I used to spend whole days with her. She played games with me and sang me songs from her childhood. I often heard her speak Piedmontese dialect with my grandfather, and in this way I had the privilege of encountering the language of their memories. Sometimes, if she had to go out, I would visit the neighbors with her. They would drink mate and chat for hours on end. Or she would take me out in the neighborhood to do her shopping. In the evening, she would take me back home to my parents, though not without first making me say my prayers. In fact, it was she who gave me my first introduction to Christianity, taught me to pray, and talked to me about that great personage I didn't yet know: Jesus.

No surprise, then, that Grandma Rosa was my godmother when I was baptized, with Francisco Sivori Sturla, my maternal grandfather, as godfather. The man who gave me that first sacrament, however, was Don Enrico Pozzoli, a fine Salesian missionary from Lodi, in Lombardy, whom my grandfather Giovanni had met in Turin. He had married my parents: they had met at a Salesian youth center in Argentina, and Don Enrico always remained a central figure for our family and my priestly vocation.

To go back to the time I spent with my grandmother: at that time I was nearly three. I was very young, so it's not easy to re-create those days in 1939, when human wickedness was unleashing another world war. My memories are like newsflashes cutting into our day-to-day life. The radio was constantly on in the background in our house: Dad would switch it on early in the morning, and he and Mom would listen to the state broadcasting station, in those days LRA 1. There were also Radio Belgrano and Radio Rivadavia, and all of them aired daily bulletins about the conflict.

My mother would also tune in on Saturday afternoons, from two o'clock on, to make us children listen to opera. She would tell us a bit about the story before it began. When there was a particularly beautiful aria, or a key turning point in the plot, she would try to get us to pay attention. I must admit we were easily distracted. We were little, after all. During Verdi's *Otello*, for example, Mom would say, "Listen carefully, this is where he kills Desdemona in her bed!" And we would fall silent, curious to hear what would happen.

To go back to the war: In our part of the world we didn't really grasp the somber mood of the time, because we were far away from the places where the fate of humanity was at stake. But I can say that, unlike many Argentines, I knew about the war because in our house it was talked about. Open letters reached us from our relatives in Italy (though with about a month's delay), and they told us what was happening. It was they who gave us news of the war in Europe. I say *open* because all mail was subject to military censorship: letters were read and resealed, and the envelopes were stamped with the words *OPENED BY CENSOR*. I remember my parents and my grandmother reading these reports out loud, and they certainly made an impression. In one letter, for example, we read that some women they knew in the town would go to Bricco Marmorito, not far from the Portacomaro railroad station, in the morning to see whether there were any military checks on the way. Their husbands hadn't gone to war; they had stayed at Bricco to work, and that, of course, was forbidden. If the women wore something red on their way back, the men would run away and hide; white clothes, on the other hand, indicated there were no patrols in the area and the men could go on working.

But that is just one example, to give an idea of the way people lived during those years. The deaths! The destruction! The boys sent to the front to die! And even though it happened more than eighty years ago, we must never forget the moments that devastated the lives of so many innocent families. War eats you up inside. You see it in the eyes of young children who no longer have any joy in their hearts, only terror and tears. The little boys and girls, let us think of them! Let us think of all those who have never breathed the scent of peace, who were born in times of war and who will live with that trauma always, carrying it within them for the rest of their lives. And what can we do for them? We should ask the question, and ask ourselves, Which is the road to peace, the way to ensure a future for those little ones?

I was alive during the war, and I was a child like them, but I was lucky because this tragedy didn't come to Argentina as it did elsewhere, apart from a few naval battles. One of the few things I do remember, partly because my parents told me about it when I was a little older, is something that happened on my third birthday. It was December 17, 1939, and we heard on the radio that a German battleship, the *Admiral Graf Spee*, had been cornered, badly damaged, by British ships near the mouth of the River Plate. Its commander, Hans Langsdorff, and his officers disobeyed Hitler's order to go on fighting and scuttled the ship. They and the crew boarded vessels bound for Buenos Aires, where in effect they surrendered to the authorities. A few days later, Langsdorff committed suicide, wrapped in the flag used by the German navy during the First World War. The other men were interned in Argentina and sent to the provinces of Córdoba and Santa Fe. I later met the son of one of those sailors, a good man who got married and started a family in Argentina.

So this was how I learned about the tragedy of the war. A few years later, when I was about ten, I encountered it through the movies too. Our parents used to take us to the local cinema to see the films that came out after the war. I saw them all. I particularly remember Roberto Rossellini's *Rome, Open City*, with Anna Magnani and Aldo Fabrizi—a masterpiece. But there were also his *Paisan* and *Germany, Year Zero*, as well as Vittorio De Sica's *The Children Are Watching Us*. These were films that shaped our consciences, and helped us understand the devastating effects of that conflict.

Federico Fellini's *La Strada*, which I saw when I was older and loved perhaps more than any other film, is quite different. It has nothing to do with the war, but I like to refer to it because in this film the director shines a spotlight on marginal figures like Gelsomina, encouraging the viewer to preserve their precious perspective on reality.

To get back to the folly of war, whose strategic plan prescribes only destruction: It makes me think about the ambition, the thirst for power, the greed that trigger conflicts. Behind them is not just ideology (an invalid justification); behind them there is also a distorted motivation, for in such times one does not look anyone in the eye—the old, children, mothers, fathers. The particular cruelty of the Second World War was even worse than that of the First. My grandfather, Giovanni Bergoglio, saw combat in that war, on the Piave River, and he told me some truly horrifying stories during my visits to the grandparental home. So many dead, so many homes destroyed—even churches. What a tragedy! He said he and his fellow soldiers at the front would sing:

General Cadorna's written to the queen:
"A postcard from Trieste will show what I've seen."
Boom boom boom
Goes the cannon . . .

As a child, I also heard the story of the war from the many migrants who came to Buenos Aires to escape the Nazi invasion of their home countries. But I'll come to that later.

Jorge does not yet grasp the drama of that global conflict: he is only three. In his innocence he does not understand the suffering of the many families forced to flee for their lives. But as he spends his days in his grandparents' home and listens to their discussions in Piedmontese dialect, he gradually becomes aware that they too, though for different reasons, have come from a place far away: Italy, from where the few remaining family members send their cousins news of the ongoing war.

In the late 1920s, after a difficult period of economic hardship, Giovanni Bergoglio decided to join the three of his six siblings who had already immigrated to Argentina. His wife, Rosa, and their son, Mario, traveled with him. Rosa had worked as a seamstress and was a leading member of Catholic Action; Mario was about twenty years old, with a diploma in accountancy. He was working in the Asti branch of the Bank of Italy. Once settled in the province of Entre Ríos, north of Buenos Aires, the Bergoglios built a successful flooring business in the city of Paraná. Thanks to the recession brought on by the crash of 1929, however, their New World dream was soon spoiled: the company was forced to close its doors in 1932. Giovanni, Rosa, and Mario, who in the meantime had started working as a bookkeeper in the family firm, had to move to Buenos Aires to make a new start. With a small loan of two thousand pesos they bought a warehouse in the working-class district of Flores, and could at last put down some roots.

Little Jorge is always asking Grandma Rosa to tell him about the long crossing on the transatlantic liner Julius Caesar, which set sail from Genoa and arrived in Buenos Aires two weeks later, on February 15, 1929. And sitting outside her front door, endlessly patient, she tells him about their arrival in the capital, dressed in clothes that were unsuited to summer in the Southern Hemisphere: she wore a coat with a fox-fur collar, in the lining of which she had sewn the family's savings.

In that September of 1939, however, when she hears the news of the outbreak of war, Rosa cannot help but think of her own relatives, the Vassallo family, who are still in the Liguria region of Italy; while

Giovanni in his shop tries every means possible to get in touch with his loved ones in Portacomaro, and the radio in the background announces that France has declared war on Germany too, confirming its alliance with the United Kingdom. Although Italy is still neutral—Benito Mussolini will not enter the war on Hitler's side until June 1940—they are tormented by worry and anxiety. Rosa occupies her day taking care of Jorge but spends hours talking to her closest friends about her former life in Italy, remembering her parents and the carefree days of her youth. Within those Argentine walls, nostalgia seems to reign supreme. And her grandson sits still, enchanted, listening to the grandmother he adores.

Grandma Rosa and Grandpa Giovanni, as well as my father, were saved by a miracle! I wouldn't be here to tell this story if their plans had not been foiled by a failed real estate sale. Their departure for Argentina was booked for October 1927; my grandfather was going to sell the family's land in Bricco, and the three of them were going to use the proceeds to board the *Princess Mafalda* at Genoa. This was a large liner that had crossed the Atlantic many times, but a broken propeller caused it to sink off the coast of Brazil on its way to Buenos Aires. More than three hundred people died: a great tragedy. Fortunately, my grandparents and my father were not on board: although the land had been put on the market some time before, there had been no offers. Without the necessary funds, therefore, and with great regret, they had had to cancel their trip a few days before departure. They had to wait till February 1929, when they boarded another ship, the *Julius Caesar*. After the two-week crossing, they arrived in Argentina and were initially housed in the Hotel de Inmigrantes, a reception center for migrants not unlike the ones we hear of today.

My father never spoke Piedmontese, perhaps because subconsciously he didn't want to acknowledge the strength of his homesickness, but my grandparents did so as a matter of course. This is why I can say that Piedmontese was my first mother tongue. I think all immigrants, during the course of their lives, find they must reckon with the same inner state as my dad. And it isn't simple! Homer speaks of this, as does the Piedmontese poet Nino Costa. I like him very much, and in one of his poems he expresses the desire to return that resides in those who cannot do so.

Migrants carry with them an enormous baggage of experience, as well as stories, that can enrich us and help us grow. As far as the war was concerned, I heard stories about that conflict in the voices of Polish immigrants. My dad worked very close to our home. He was the accountant for an industrial dyeworks, which dyed yarns and fabrics for large clients. A few at a time, Polish workers started arriving. They had seen the war with their own eyes, the invasion of Nazi troops, the death of loved ones. They had experienced the drama and had fled to South America, driven by the dream of a new life. When I went to see Dad at work—by this time I was eight or nine—I would sometimes stay and listen to their stories. They were fine people, those Poles, maybe ten of them, with big hearts. Their stories were very distressing, because they were talking of shattered families, friends sent to the front never to return, mothers who expected to welcome their beloved children back with a hug but received only flowers after the deaths of their sons.

I must say, though, that those people had not lost the capacity to laugh, despite the traumas they had experienced. Sometimes they would take us children aside and teach us a few swear words in Polish as a prank. I remember one of them saying to me, "Go over to that lady and say this word to her." Obviously the word meant nothing to me, but in Polish it certainly wasn't a compliment!

So there were lighter moments alongside the stories of war. But you could see in their eyes the characteristic nostalgia of people who have been forced to leave their homes. It is a thorn in the heart. And how many more, even today, find themselves having to run away in hope of a new life—just like my grandparents and those Polish immigrants—but find only death at sea or rejection at the border. Once again, it is human wickedness that causes these dramas, it is the hardened hearts of people who do not embrace the gospel, which tells us to open the door when someone knocks, to open our hearts when someone needs a warm place or an outstretched hand to raise them up.

Think how many Italians left for South America or the United States before and after the war. Think how many of our own relatives were migrants. Even they, perhaps, were thought of as the "bad" or "dangerous" ones in the countries where they landed. But in fact they were just trying to make a future for their children. "Where is Abel your brother?" the Lord asks Cain, in the book of Genesis. It is a question that resonates today, and leaves us disoriented. We neglect that which God has created, and we are no longer capable of taking care of each other. And when this disorientation infects the whole world, tragedies like the ones we keep reading about in the papers will happen.

I want to repeat this, I want to shout it out: Please, let us welcome our brothers and sisters when they knock at our door. Because if they are properly integrated, if they are supported and looked after, they can make a big contribution to our lives. Like those Polish immigrants I knew as a child, who had fled the war, today's migrants are just people looking for a better place who often find death instead. Too often, sadly, these brothers and sisters of ours, who want a little peace, encounter neither welcome nor solidarity, only an accusing finger. It is prejudice that corrupts the soul; it is wickedness that kills. And it is a dead end, a perversion. Let us not forget, for example, what happened to our Jewish brothers and sisters. And in their case, too, memories are plentiful.

II

THE EXTERMINATION
OF THE JEWS

Paradies Lagardère - GSO
Greensboro #0642 CNBC News

500142 Patrick D   Till: 064201

\# 10234   03/25/2024 04:25 PM

                                          USD
LIFE   28.99
    7018502

                              Subtotal: 28.99
                                 Taxes: 1.96

Total USD   30.95

4 MASTERCARD   30.95

Reprint # 1
Thank you for shopping Paradies Lagardère
Piedmont Triad International Airport
Greensboro, NC
Visit Us on the Web!
WWW.PARADIESLAGARDERE.COM

*************** PURCHASE ***************
               APPROVED
Total: $30.95
Card Type: MASTERCARD
Card Entry: CHIP
Acct #:   ************6581
Approval Code: 011544
************* EMV PURCHASE *************
App Label: Mastercard Debit
Mode: Issuer
AID: A0000000041010
TVR: 0000008000
IAD: 011060700122000065E400000000000000FF
TSI: E800
ARC: 00
AC: AE8FE529336C7B0B
CVM: 1E0300

"He really is a monster, there's no other word." Gesturing angrily, Jorge's mother, Regina, stands up from the table, abandoning her bowl of soup. For her at least, supper seems to be over. Still thinking about what her mother-in-law has just told her, she slams the pan of leftover soup down in the sink, sending it splattering all over, while repeatedly saying, "What a monster!"

Marta, the youngest, frightened by her mother's tone of voice, bursts into tears; her two older brothers, Jorge and Oscar, who are fighting a duel with their spoons instead of eating, stop, shocked into silence. Jorge, in particular, looks curiously at his mother, while their father, Mario, stands and picks up Marta. He has never seen his wife so angry. It may have happened in the past, because of some wrong done to her, but never because of an item of news that does not affect her personally. The atmosphere in the Bergoglio house is not at its best on that warm evening in December 1941. After an emotional few minutes, everything falls suddenly silent: the only sound is that of water running in the sink, mingled with Regina's tears. And then the occasional shout of a child *playing outside in the street, accompanied by the gradually dwindling rumble of a clapped-out old truck taking a group of night workers off to their jobs outside Flores.*

It is Grandma Rosa who has set off this reaction in her daughter-in-law, after a visit that afternoon from an old friend who immigrated to Argentina from Turin. Signora Margherita Muso Nero—it means black snout, and it really is her name—told Rosa the latest news from Italy. Many of her relatives fled abroad when the Racial Laws were passed in 1938, while others stayed behind in the hope that this time would sooner or later pass into memory. In the latest letter they reported what they had heard: persecution was already happening in other countries, and, alongside the construction of ghettos in big cities occupied by the Nazis, thousands of people had died. Many people were being taken away by force—a long way away, to labor camps. In reality, what was happening would later be known as the Final Solution: entire communities shot to death, mobile gas chambers, and, above all, deportations to the main concentration camps—Auschwitz was already in operation by 1940, while Auschwitz II–Birkenau reached that stage in October 1941.

Eyes glistening, Rosa listened carefully to her friend's report, which described Jews boarding trains to an unknown destination, loaded by force into cars designed to carry animals, not human beings. Hundreds of people crowded on top of one another, with their suitcases and their lives' memories beside them. Children torn from their mothers or hidden with neighbors, husbands separated from their other halves, their legs beaten with sticks to make them walk faster.

After her friend's visit, a little before that supper with its starter of soup, Grandma brought Jorge home and stayed a while to whisper to her son and daughter-in-law what Signora Muso Nero had told her. Rosa's character is forthright, decisive; she did not want the children to hear these sad stories, so she switched on the radio and turned the volume up higher than usual. The notes of a tango suddenly streamed into the dining room: Radio El Mundo was playing "Recuerdo" (Memory) by Osvaldo Pugliese, known in Buenos Aires as the patron saint of tango. And little Jorge, nearly five years old, seemed to enjoy it. That music in the background gave his grandmother's dramatic tale a soundtrack that freighted her words with even more emotion. Mario's thoughts flew to his Jewish friends, and he uttered the word, monster, that would be repeated a few minutes later, at supper, by his wife.

I heard it often at home during that period: "Hitler's a monster!" It would come up at supper or lunch, or when an uncle or cousin came to visit. My parents obviously weren't indifferent to what was happening in Europe, and they would say the man's name when they were talking to each other or to my grandmother. I was too young to understand. Later, when I was a little older, I understood who the monster was.

My father worked with many Jews at the time, some of whom became friends. Several customers of the dyeworks, people who sent their yarn or stockings to be dyed, belonged to the Jewish community. Occasionally they would visit him at home, with their whole families in tow. Naturally, the persecution of Jews would come up in conversation, since these gentlemen had relatives scattered all over Europe, and some of them, unfortunately, had been taken away and never heard from again.

While the grown-ups talked about these things, we children would go and play with a ball outside, or in another room. It was the same at my grandmother's house. Signora Muso Nero, an ordinary, decent woman, often came to visit, though she was at least ten years younger, and she would tell my grandmother about her relatives and what they were going through.

At my grandmother's, too, the children were asked to go away, so that these conversations wouldn't upset us. But from time to time I did catch a few words—the names my grandmother called Hitler! and also the people in our country who supported him! For in Argentina in those days there was a minority that was anti-Semitic. I don't mean everyone, of course, but some fringe groups had espoused the ideals of the Third Reich, particularly some who are close to nationalism. Even in our part of the world, therefore, there were feelings of hostility toward the Jewish people, and this has always wounded me.

I have often asked the Lord to forgive these people, and the cruelty of totalitarian regimes; I wrote it in the Book of Honor when I visited the Auschwitz and Birkenau camps in Poland in 2016. It was a silent pilgrimage: I didn't make any speeches. Words would have been superfluous in the face of that appalling tragedy. At the wall where prisoners were executed with a shot to the head, I was moved to pray for the souls of the victims, for these our older brothers and sisters in faith, and for every community that has suffered the atrocity of this human madness. I also visited the starvation cell where St. Maximilian Kolbe was held. He was a Franciscan friar who offered his own life in place of that of another prisoner, a man with a family. Something that has always caused me pain is that these people, who were guilty of nothing, were led to this place by trickery. They thought they were going to labor camps; they didn't know that within a very short time they would be murdered. I uttered no words during my visits to the concentration and extermination camps, but I can say, so many years later, that inside them the air you breathe still smells of death and cruelty. It was frightening.

Going back to that period in the 1940s, when the Nazis decided to wipe out the Jews, Signora Muso Nero's reports brought home to my grandmother the depth of the tragedy and also provided explanations that I could use in the years that followed. The fact is that at the age of five or six it would have been impossible for me to understand that human beings could go so far, or to understand what would happen as a result. I have become fully aware of this drama, thanks to my teachers at school, my family, the study of history, and above all thanks to the stories of survivors who over the years have told me of their experiences of imprisonment in those death camps, places where human dignity was utterly crushed.

I have heard many such stories, some of them from my friend Rabbi Abraham Skorka, but I will mention only two.

The first is the story of Lidia Maksymowicz, the daughter of two partisans in Byelorussia, whom I met in the Vatican. She was only three years old when she was deported and marked with a tattoo by the Nazis. Members of her family were interned as political prisoners, because her parents had openly sided with the Jews from the start, though they were not themselves Jewish. Lidia was assigned to the Auschwitz II–Birkenau camp in 1943, separated from her mother and, along with many other children, subjected to the experiments of Dr. Josef Mengele. This man did terrible things. He tested drugs and poisons on them, treating them as young guinea pigs. Poor little things. We were together for a few minutes after the general audience, and on this occasion too I didn't say a word, apart from a simple *thank you* for her testimony. And in a spontaneous gesture I kissed the tattooed number she had borne on her arm since the age of three.

The second is the story of another survivor, Edith Bruck, a Hungarian Jew whose stories and courage greatly impressed me. Amid the darkness of the camp she was able to find some light. At Dachau a Nazi cook asked her name and, seeing how young and defenseless she was, said, "I have a daughter like you." And he gave her a comb, even though her head had been shaved. A sign of hope in that ocean of death. When I visited her at home in Rome, she told me this story, and I said, "I would like to have been that cook." But I also asked her forgiveness for everything that happened to the Jews. I met Edith in public on other occasions, in Rome, and one more time in private, in the Vatican, always on January 27, Holocaust Remembrance Day.

Remembrance: these people are living memorials, a priceless treasure for us all. The extermination of millions of Jews must not be forgotten and must never be repeated. No more genocide, no more cruelty. The Shoah teaches us that maximum vigilance is required if we don't want to arrive too late when the peace and dignity of human beings are under attack.

The tango on the radio, which briefly distracted little Jorge while his parents and Grandma Rosa were talking, is interrupted by the seven o'clock news: the newsreader announces the Japanese attack on the American base at Pearl Harbor, Hawaii, at dawn on Sunday, December 7, 1941. Thousands are dead, mainly military personnel. Up to that moment, most Americans have been against any intervention in the war, but after Pearl Harbor the situation changes radically, and President Franklin Delano Roosevelt announces the entry of the United States into the war, alongside Great Britain and the Soviet Union. Everyone falls abruptly silent at the news. Rosa clasps her hands together and shakes her head in resignation, as if to say, That's all we need. She says a hasty goodbye: it's late, and she has to cook supper for her husband, Giovanni.

"See you tomorrow, eh?" she says to Jorge, giving him a kiss. She will be walking him to Our Lady of Mercy infant school, in Avenida Directorio, not far from home. It is a convent school, and Jorge has been going there for more than a year.

Regina is back at the stove, putting the finishing touches to the first course. Mario has taken his account books off the table: even on a Sunday he has brought work home. Now he gathers the children together and makes them wash their hands and then sit down at the table, while he and his wife discuss Rosa's stories about the Jews.

"How did we get to this?" they ask, not going into detail so as not to distress the children.

"He obviously thinks he's a god," says Regina, visibly upset, as she carries the pan to the table.

"Poor things," Mario goes on. "They must have been so frightened during that train journey, especially the children. I wonder what happened when they reached their destination."

"Dad? What train journey?" the children ask in unison, but there is no reply.

After a few spoonfuls of soup, Regina is unable to hold it back any longer, as she thinks about the Jewish children separated from their mothers. For no reason.

"He really is a monster, there's no other word!" she bursts out.

Because they had young children themselves, our parents were very sensitive to anything bad that happened to others of our age. When it came to deportations of Jews, young or old, their sensitivity was even higher. As devout, practicing Christians, they couldn't accept what was happening, which is why they applied this label to Hitler. And they weren't wrong.

When I read in the papers about cases of anti-Semitism or racism arising today, I sometimes feel as if I am reliving those emotions. Consider, for example, the acts of violence committed by a few fanatics, the desecration of Jewish graves or the houses daubed with the star of David in various European countries after the outbreak of the new conflict in the Middle East in October 2023. It's shameful, particularly as it often involves the young. As if they didn't understand what the Shoah was.

Let us also think about people with dark skin. In the United States, for example, there continue to be big demonstrations over the deaths of Black citizens, victims of a very specific prejudice. The story of George Floyd, and other Americans like him, has had considerable resonance. But this is not just a problem for the United States; it affects European countries too.

Fortunately there is always a collective reaction against social or racial injustice, against abuse of power, whenever human dignity is wounded. For this reason I like to define nonviolent protestors as collective good Samaritans, intervening to defend the dignity of human beings, all human beings. But let us remember that racism is a disease, a virus; the case of Hitler is a disease multiplied to the umpteenth power, because he eliminated not only Jews but also Roma, people with disabilities, homosexuals, the old, even children with Down syndrome. He sent them all to their deaths, without pity. This has always caused me pain inside. I have never come to terms with it. This is why I say we cannot turn a blind eye to cases of anti-Semitism, racism, or discrimination. We must defend the sanctity of human life. The name of God is profaned and defiled in the madness of hate. It happens today and it happened in the criminal actions of the regime during World War II. History repeats itself. We see it every day, for example in what is happening in Ukraine and the Middle East.

The Jewish community living far from Europe really suffered during the years of my childhood: I could glimpse it in the eyes of my father's friends when they visited, and in their children's eyes. Some of them lived with a permanent weight on their hearts, even when they were playing with me. Perhaps they knew something about what was happening to their people and relatives, because they hardly ever smiled, and their expressions were sad. And I see this today, when I receive children who have come away from war zones. Their eyes do not smile: their smiles are always forced.

Children, with their innocence, can teach us a lot, especially in these times of war. This is one of the reasons why I wanted to create a World Day dedicated to them—so that they could be our principal "allies" in the search for peace. With their pure and simple hearts they tell us so much, mainly because they are already educated in peace at school. Every time I come into contact with them I go back to being a child myself a little, in my heart, and I forget all the difficulties and arguments that come up as I carry out my duties. When I look at them, so happy and full of life, I see again the enthusiasm of me and my friends playing in the street. There were arguments, of course, and the occasional rude word would slip out, but in the end we always made peace . . . and had a delicious snack made by Grandma Rosa: bread and sugar.

In remembrance of all the Jews who suffered and paid with their lives for the fact of belonging to their people, in 2014 I paid a visit to Yad Vashem, the World Holocaust Remembrance Center, in Jerusalem. In my address, I asked some simple questions: "Who are you, o man? What have you become? Of what horror have you been capable? What made you fall to such depths? . . . Who convinced you that you were God? Not only did you torture and kill your brothers and sisters, but you sacrificed them to yourself, because you made yourself a god. . . . Almighty Lord, . . . Remember us in your mercy. Grant us the grace to be ashamed of what we men have done, to be ashamed of this massive idolatry, of having despised and destroyed our own flesh which you formed from the earth, to which you gave life with your own breath of life. Never again, Lord, never again!"

So we must not forget that the past century saw so much brutality against the Jewish people. We thought it was finished when the war ended and the Nazi regime collapsed, but Jews continue to be stereotyped and persecuted. This is not Christian; it's not even human. When will we understand that these are our brothers and sisters?

I cannot conceal that my thoughts often go back to all those people suffering and dying in the camps in the 1940s while we were living peacefully and worry-free in our homes in Argentina. We had everything, though we lived simply. It wasn't important to own a car or a custom-made suit, to go on vacation—the important thing was to be happy. And that, thanks be to God, was never lacking in our family. Above all, we didn't have to live with the fear that the SS would come knocking and ransack our home; there were no Nazi patrols in the street; mothers weren't having their heads shaved, being separated from their children, and getting sent to camps, wearing only a filthy coverall, stripped of all dignity. Nor were men being compelled into forced labor and then, when they were no longer useful, being murdered and thrown into incinerators.

Why did they go through this and not me? Why were so many children, just like me, separated from their parents, while my siblings and I were given the heaven-sent gift of a happy childhood? I ask the question with my heart in pieces, but I haven't found the answer yet.

III

ATOM BOMBS AND
THE END OF THE WAR

The stadium is ecstatic. The referee, Eduardo Forte, has blown the final whistle, and the fans are celebrating at the tops of their voices, dancing and singing in praise of the terceto de oro, the golden trio of Armando Farro, René Pontoni, and Rinaldo Fioramonte Martino. Even in Farro's absence, the match has ended 6-1 to the blue-and-reds against Ferro Carril Oeste, the team from the Caballito district. An extraordinary result on a historic day: September 2, 1945. Nobody expected a result like this from San Lorenzo, not even their coach, Diego García, and yet the miracle has happened. Among the most fiercely loyal San Lorenzo fans in the terraces is the whole Bergoglio family. Mario has brought Regina and his four children: Jorge, sitting beside his father, Oscar, Marta, and little Alberto, now three years old.

Pontoni and his teammates make a circuit of the pitch, waving to the crowd, but there is a special reason for celebration. Before the match, the radio announced that a Japanese delegation headed by Minister of Foreign Affairs Mamoru Shigemitsu, in the presence of General Douglas MacArthur, had signed the instrument of surrender aboard the US battleship *Missouri* just off the port of Yokohama. This made it official: the war had ended. In Europe the fighting had been over for some months: faced with British, American, and Russian troops advancing on Berlin, Hitler committed suicide on April 30; on May 7, Germany signed its unconditional surrender to the Allied forces at Reims, in France.

But the surrender on September 2, 1945, marks the end of all hostilities everywhere, as the world mourns the victims of the two atomic bombs dropped on the Japanese cities of Hiroshima and Nagasaki by the United States. More than 200,000 dead and 150,000 injured. Even in Argentina people are celebrating the end of the war, and everyone is talking about these new weapons: in bars, in the newspapers, on the radio, at church, among neighbors. Jorge, now nearly nine, hears his parents talking about them, but also his teacher at the Escuela Primaria 8 Coronel Ingeniero Pedro Antonio Cerviño, which he attends daily. A good pupil, he wears a white smock with a black scarf tied in a bow. His teacher, Estela Quiroga, is struck by the boy's unusual methods. For example, rather than writing things down or counting on his fingers when studying arithmetic, he practices addition, subtraction, and multiplication by climbing up and down the school stairs. Besides mathematics, he enjoys reading, stamp collecting, and sports. He plays basketball with his father, kicks a ball around with his neighborhood friends, and then, every Sunday, goes to the football stadium with his family.

Before that extraordinary San Lorenzo match on Sunday, September 2, 1945, Jorge went with Grandma Rosa to morning mass in the San José de Flores basilica, ten minutes from the house. Then he came home and played cards (briscola) with Oscar and their parents. In the back-

ground, Beethoven's Leonore Overture No. 3: Mario had put on a record of Fidelio, setting aside the account books he had brought home as usual to finish the week's work. Although he earns less than his colleagues— his Italian qualification is not recognized in Argentina—he always has a smile on his face, especially when he has to chide his children when they don't understand the rules of briscola.

But the relaxed atmosphere did not last forever: when the clock said eleven-thirty, it was time for Mom and Dad to get to work at the stove. But someone outside was shouting Regina's name, interrupting the enjoyable calm of the family's morning.

It was our neighbor, María, who was urgently calling my mother. I remember that day in September 1945 as if it were yesterday. Our house was separated from the neighbors' by a wall several feet high. All the properties in the neighborhood were separated like this. The lady who lived next door was standing on her side of the wall shouting my mother's name to get her out of the house: "Señora Regina! Señora Regina!" My mother went out immediately, thinking something bad had happened. And the woman shouted again, this time with a beautiful smile on her face: "Señora Regina! The war's over!" My mother was confused for a moment, then they both burst into tears of joy. Liberating tears. Meanwhile, the daily newspaper *La Prensa* had sounded its siren, an extremely loud noise that was used to warn the public when something significant happened. It was so powerful it sounded as if it were just around the corner, when in fact the paper's offices were five or six miles away. People came out onto their balconies and into the streets to see what was happening. My brothers and my dad did the same. It was a very emotional moment. Having witnessed the scene, which I can still see clearly in my mind's eye, I can say that I learned an important lesson that day: I learned how much these simple people, though they lived in South America and therefore far away from the theater of war, yearned for peace. The wonderful feeling we all had was that of a terrible nightmare coming to an end at last, especially when we remembered the poor souls who had died or had been forced to flee—some to our part of the world.

Clearly we were all, everywhere, anxiously waiting for news of the end of the war. History repeats itself, and what happened then is happening now too: we are all suffering because of the conflict and violence affecting various parts of the planet, and we wonder what we can do to relieve people's suffering. We can contribute through charitable works, of course, like reconstruction or the distribution of vital aid, but our most significant contribution may be the effort to eradicate from our hearts any hatred and resentment for those who live alongside us. We are all brothers and sisters, and there must be no resentment among us. For any war to truly end, forgiveness is necessary. Otherwise what will follow is not justice but revenge.

We must learn to build a culture of peace in this world. This should not be seen only through the lens of rejecting the violence of weapons; let us also think about the violence of our destructive rumor-mongering, let us think about psychological violence toward people who are weak and defenseless, let us think about the violence of the abuse of power, even within the Church. Do we really want peace? If so, let us start by working on ourselves. St. Paul shows us the way, teaching us that mercy, benevolence, and forgiveness are the best medicines we can use to build a culture of peace.

I am reminded of the words of Pope Pius XII, broadcast on the radio in August 1939, on the eve of war. We heard it at home: "Nothing is lost with peace; all may be lost with war. Let men return to mutual understandings. Let them begin negotiations anew. Let them confer with goodwill and with respect for reciprocal rights. They will find that an honorable result is never impossible through sincere and effective negotiations."

But human wickedness, then as now, didn't have ears to listen to these wise and pious words. Just six years later, in August 1945, two atomic bombs destroyed Hiroshima and Nagasaki. I remember people talking about this catastrophic event. In the bar, or in the Salesian youth centers, they said the Americans—they called them *los gringos*—had launched these murderous weapons, but nobody really understood. We children certainly didn't understand, but nor did the adults. "What is an atomic bomb? How does it work?" everyone wanted to know. And there were detailed explanations of the science in the papers and on the radio: how the explosion was triggered, what happened to the atoms, the destructive power of this weapon. Some people even wondered whether the radioactive effects could somehow reach South America or Argentina. People didn't have the knowledge they do today, and there was a lot of fear in the air. Fear and despair: I have heard dramatic stories from the mouths of people who were at Hiroshima, during and after the detonation of the bomb. But I'll talk about that later.

The end of the war is being celebrated out in the streets of Buenos Aires too. Mario switches on the radio to catch any updates; Regina has gone back into the kitchen to make lunch. They are in a hurry because they are going to the San Lorenzo match in the early afternoon, and it will take a while to get to the stadium, especially without a car. Fortunately, Grandma Rosa has arrived to help: she and Giovanni will eat with them. The children are playing in the living room. Oscar is proudly showing Jorge his prize, two coins his father gave him after the game of briscola. Marta tries to snatch one from his hands. She is curious, she wants to touch a coin. And then there is a squabble, with screams, tears, pulled hair.

"Go on, Oscar, give her one. She just wants to look at it. She'll give it back," says Grandma.

"No, she wants to keep it. She'll just go and hide it somewhere," the child replies sulkily.

"But that won't be a problem. It will mean you've given it to her. Remember: the shroud has no pockets. It's pointless to be attached to money," Grandma explains.

The children fall silent, but Jorge is struck by his grandmother's words. He understands what they mean and gestures to Oscar to give one of his coins to his little sister. Marta is satisfied and, having kissed her brother, goes back to her room to play.

The sports bulletin, broadcast in the buildup to the afternoon's match, is now over, and, as the family prepares ravioli, there is a news report on the day's events. It shows celebrations in the streets of Washington, London, and Paris; the responses of governments all over the world; the arrival of American soldiers in Tokyo, where they received bouquets of flowers from Japanese children. Everywhere, people are breathing the air of peace. But still unfolding is the dramatic story of the two atomic bombs and the effects of thermal radiation on the

populace, who are being treated mainly in the Japanese Empire's field
hospitals. One part of the world is partying; the other part is counting
the dead and wounded. A reporter tells of a woman who was wearing
a kimono when the bomb exploded. The radiation was so powerful that
the pattern of the fabric was imprinted on her back, like a tattoo.

Mario switches the radio off abruptly. The details are becoming un-
suitable for children. Besides, fortunately, it is time to come to the table.

Terrible news kept coming in from Japan. On the radio they were
talking about all the people who had survived the explosions but
were left with nothing and would probably die soon because of the
radiation. Everyone in our own neighborhood was talking about
it too. There was real fear that it could happen again, that another
sudden flash of light could swallow everything up anew, with no escape for anyone.

Though I was physically far away, in a certain sense I experienced
this tragedy close up, thanks to the stories of Father Pedro Arrupe,
who happened to pass through Argentina several years later, when
I was a young Jesuit student. He was a missionary in Hiroshima,
rector of the Jesuit novitiate there, and had miraculously escaped
the explosion, along with the thirty-five young men who lived at the
institution and some other Jesuits. However, he never said it was a
miracle, even though the bomb detonated very close to the Society
of Jesus building.

But he did tell me that, on the day of the attack on August 6,
1945, he heard a powerful explosion and everything was smashed to
pieces. Doors, walls, furniture flew away in fragments. He and the

others managed to escape through fields of rice. From the safety of a hilltop they could see that the whole city had been razed to the ground. His description was terrifying: he saw a huge lake of fire, and countless incinerated bodies.

Father Pedro had studied medicine. In the absence of doctors, since they had almost all been killed, he was able to give a helping hand where it was needed. He turned the novitiate into a field hospital. It was a good idea, but they were short of drugs. Luckily, a farmer gave him a sack containing about fifty pounds of powdered boric acid, and this, dissolved in water, allowed Father Pedro to treat a large number of burn wounds. Aid from nearby cities didn't start arriving until the following day, but the strength of the Japanese was incredible. They recovered and started rebuilding immediately. As an adult and a Jesuit, I would have liked to do missionary work in Japan myself, but I was refused permission on account of my health, which was a little precarious at the time. Who knows, if they had sent me on a mission there, my life might have taken a different turn, and maybe some people in the Vatican would have been happier!

During those terrible days, Father Arrupe continued to help survivors, but he also sought donations to rebuild the Jesuit buildings, begging for charity door to door. There was great generosity in the midst of suffering. While he was living among so many despairing people, however, others were raising their glasses in celebration of victory. The use of atomic energy for purposes of war is a crime against humanity, against human dignity, and against any possibility of a future in our shared home. It is immoral! How can we hold ourselves up as champions of peace and justice if at the same time we are building new weapons of war? The possession of these weapons of mass destruction only gives us a false sense of security, because what they create is an atmosphere of suspicion and fear. The use of such bombs would also have a catastrophic environmental and humanitarian effect. Let us remember what happened in Japan! I went there in 2019 and visited the Hiroshima Peace Memorial. It was a truly moving experience, thinking of all those innocent victims. I wanted to undertake this pilgrimage mainly to reassert three moral imperatives that might open the way to peace: to remember, to journey together, to protect. We must not allow generations to come, as well as today's, to lose the memory of what happened, a living memory that can help generation after generation to say: never again!

To this end we must walk in unity, with our gaze fixed on forgiveness, shining a beam of light among the many clouds that obscure the sky these days. And there are so many, if we look at the "hot" zones of the planet and the way our brothers and sisters live in tormented Ukraine, Syria, Yemen, Myanmar, the Middle East, South Sudan—and all the other places where the tragedy of war is still being lived. Instead, we must be open to hope and be the instruments of peace and reconciliation. We will succeed in this if we are able to protect each other, and recognize each other as brothers and sisters with a common destiny. Let us therefore raise a cry from our hearts, today as back then: no more war, no more thundering guns, no more of such suffering. Let there be peace for everyone. A lasting peace without weapons.

Even when I was at school, back in 1945, there was much talk of the end of the war and how the great powers had carved up the world among them. I remember that we students did projects on the subject of peace, and I enjoyed that.

The subject still attracted a lot of attention in the years that followed, when I changed schools. My youngest sister, María Elena, was born in 1948. My mother's health was poor, and she could no longer take care of us all, so in 1949, Oscar, Marta, and I, with the help of Don Pozzoli, were sent to Salesian boarding schools. Marta, who was eight years old, went to the girls' school, St. Mary Help of Christians, while my brother and I went to the Wilfrid Barón de los Santos Ángeles school in Ramos Mejía, about seven miles from our home.

I was in sixth grade, and I must say I never had time to be bored. We were plunged into a life where there really was no room for idleness: We started early in the morning with mass, study, lessons; we played during recesses; and then, at the end of the day, we listened to the director's goodnight talk. I learned how to study, because the teachers taught me memory techniques I use to this day. And then the silence: it was wonderful to study for hours and hours, immersed in absolute silence, because it helped concentration. We also did a lot of sports because this, they said, was a fundamental part of life. After so much anxiety about the war and the atomic bombs, activities that offered distraction were essential, as long as they were limited to healthy competition. They taught us to compete like Christians: no foul play, therefore, and truthfulness on the playing field above all!

But I think the most important thing was that the college, by awakening our consciousness to the truth of things, built a Catholic culture that was neither bigoted nor directionless. We lived our piety toward others, and it was real. This created habits that, taken together, molded a way of being that actually followed Catholic teaching. There, for example, I learned to open up to others, to deprive myself of some things in order to give them to someone poorer than me. After all, the shroud has no pockets, remember?

So it's not surprising that it was among the Salesians, at the age of twelve, that I first sensed my vocation as a priest. I plucked up the courage to talk about it with Father Martínez, familiar to us all because he was known as *el pescador*, the fisherman, for the large number of vocations he had uncovered among the boys at Salesian schools. I met with him a few times, he asked me some questions, gave me some advice, but our conversations never went very deep. The desire was still dormant within me, and didn't erupt definitively until the 1950s.

IV

THE COLD WAR
AND McCARTHYISM

"Good morning, Jorge, what a lovely surprise! What brings you here? It's not summer yet."

The unmistakable voice of Esther rings out in the still-deserted rooms of the Hickethier-Bachmann Laboratory, where the teenage Jorge Bergoglio has unexpectedly appeared at seven o'clock on a cold and rainy morning in June 1953 (the seasons are reversed in Argentina, since it is in the Southern Hemisphere).

By this time the boy is a familiar presence. They know him well, because he has been getting real-world work experience every summer (December to March) at this center for chemical analysis in the Recoleta district of Buenos Aires. His job is to carry out quality control on foodstuffs.

His father, Mario, insisted. He wants his son to get experience of the world of work during the hot season, so Jorge rolled up his sleeves. Managing his work at the lab alongside his studies is hard for him, but he is not the only one who emerges exhausted at the end of each day. Practical experience in the real world, in a factory or a laboratory, is required by the institution he is now attending: Industrial School number 12. For all students in years three, four, and five, the summer program is divided into lessons in theory in the afternoon, between two and six, and practice in the morning, from seven till one. Only an hour's break, just long enough to make the trip from the laboratory to the school, with a sandwich clenched between the teeth. After seven years, this will culminate in a diploma as qualified chemist.

But Jorge's unexpected visit, this winter morning, has nothing to do with his studies: before going into class, the sixteen-year-old just wants to say hello and have a chat with the head of the lab.

Her name is Esther Ballestrino; she is a thirty-five-year-old Paraguayan biochemist who fled her country in the face of persecution under the dictatorship of General Higinio Morínigo Martínez. She is, in fact, a Marxist activist, a member of the Revolutionary Febrerista Party, a leading figure in the defense of rural women and workers. Her words and actions are not tolerated by the Paraguayan authorities, and Esther was forced to take refuge in the Argentina of Juan Domingo and Evita Perón.

Alternating between kindness and severity, this stylish young woman, with her rich chestnut-colored hair, has taught Jorge how to use a microscope and a range of chemical apparatus, but what she really enjoys is talking with him about current affairs, what is going on in the world, Marxist thought, and workers' rights—even outside working hours.

Her office door is always open: she is surrounded by bulky folders and testing equipment. On her desk, in addition to piles of papers and test results to be sent out to clients, there is always a daily newspaper. Esther buys it at the newsstand every morning and reads it during her breaks. That morning, the foreign news includes a report on the execution by electric chair of Julius and Ethel Rosenberg at Sing Sing prison. They were condemned to death two years earlier, convicted of spying for the Soviet Union. According to the judge, the couple had passed top-secret information about nuclear weapons to the Soviets.

"Listen to this, Jorge," Esther says, to catch the boy's attention, and starts reading the article out loud. "They had to give the poor woman more shocks than usual, because she wouldn't die. That's what the Cold War has done," she adds. "Or rather, that's one of the cruelest results of McCarthyism."

That word, McCarthyism, is not new to Jorge: he has heard it used by a few teachers, referring to a 1950 cartoon by Herbert Block ("Herblock") in the Washington Post, which used the term for the first time and made it famous all over the world.

The United States is going through a period of rising social tensions caused by a commission set up by Senator Joseph McCarthy to root out the "un-American activities" of suspected communists, men and women whose ideology might undermine the foundations of American society. In its sights are artists, journalists, writers, cultural figures both male and female, members of the armed forces, and government officials. There starts to be talk of "witch-hunts"; the "Red Scare" seems to be at the top of the agenda, while the two principal power blocs, American and Soviet, are further apart than ever. Faced with this scenario, the Peronist Argentina of the descamisados (the shirtless) decides to distance itself from the historical influence of the United States and stay out of the Cold War: it announces a third way, neither capitalist nor communist.

From the point of view of international politics, this was a very "hot" period. The Cold War was hitting many people in the wallet, which sparked very provocative public statements, protests, suspicions, and often reprisals. I remember many satirical cartoons in Argentine newspapers representing the United States and the Soviet Union as two giants conducting an underground war, without visible weapons but with threats and espionage.

There were also stories about the struggle for power in the Soviet Union after the death of Stalin, an episode I remember clearly: some people talked of freedom, while others felt great sadness. Nostalgic for Stalinism! I am reminded, too, of the Rosenbergs, a nasty business that developed in that atmosphere of suspicion, of McCarthyism, amid the hunt for communist spies on American soil.

I remember that the pope—it was Pius XII at the time—asked in a message that the couple be spared the death penalty. For the Church, no matter how long it has gone on, and no matter how much it persists to this day in so many countries of the world, the death penalty is inadmissible. Even for a person who is convicted of a crime, there must be a window of hope, whereas capital punishment represents the defeat of justice. People can redeem themselves to the last, they can change. This practice doesn't allow for that possibility; it destroys the most important gift we have received from the Lord: life. And I ask myself: Who are these people to decide to deprive others of life? Maybe they wish to take the place of God! I want to reaffirm that, today more than ever, we need a collective spiritual mobilization of all Christians to give concrete support to organizations that are fighting for the abolition of the death penalty. In this we must be united!

In the 1950s, McCarthyism in the United States was a marginal subject in Argentine society. It was discussed at the level of newspaper articles and television debates, but we had problems in our own domestic politics to resolve. While I did do some reading of a political nature during those years, like most young people of my age I had other things on my mind, such as meeting up with friends, hunting out new books at knockdown prices, or playing sports. I can say, though, that the story of the Rosenbergs, and the social phenomenon of the United States, were well explained to me by Esther, the head of my laboratory.

Esther was a remarkable woman, and I owe her a great deal. Yes, she was a communist through and through, and an atheist, but a respectful one: although she had her own beliefs, she never attacked faith, not even when she was talking privately with friends. And she taught me so much about politics. Around that time she gave me some publications, including that of the communist party, *Nuestra Palabra* (Our Word) and *Propósitos* (Intentions). I was very keen on the articles by Leónidas Barletta, an Argentine writer and director, a prominent figure in the independent left. Nevertheless, I never embraced communist ideology: my reading of these things was on an intellectual level only, as well as being a way for me to understand the world that Esther came from.

After my election as pope, some people claimed I spoke about the poor so often because I was a communist or a Marxist myself. A cardinal friend of mine once even told me that one lady, a good Catholic, had told him she was convinced that Pope Francis was the anti-pope. Why? Because I don't wear the papal red shoes! But talking about the poor doesn't necessarily mean one is a communist: the poor are the flag of the gospel and are in Jesus's heart. Poverty has no ideology; the Church has none either, and shouldn't: as I say so often, it isn't a parliament! Not everything can be reduced to factions on the right or left. In chapter 4, verse 32, of the Acts of the Apostles, for example, we read, "Now the company of those who believed were of one heart and soul, and no one said that any of the things which he possessed was his own, but they had everything in common." So in the earliest Christian communities property was shared. It's not communism; it's Christianity in its purest form.

For her part, Esther explained that it was important to be clear-eyed and wise in order to discern and understand why people talked about the communist threat to American democracy. Was the specter of communism being used as a means to an end? Or was there really a danger that state secrets would be given away? These were questions that many people asked in those days.

Many years after our conversations, Esther embarked on a painful struggle when she founded the Mothers of the Plaza de Mayo, a group of distraught mothers of the *desaparecidos* (the disappeared). She founded this group in the San Cristóbal district, in the parish of Santa Cruz, where this dear friend of mine is now buried. But I will say more on this later.

A dear friend she was, yes, but she certainly gave me a hard time! At work she was extremely rigorous: if I brought her the results of an analysis too quickly, she would become suspicious and make me do it again. Alternatively, if I didn't carry out a test because I thought it was pointless, she would insist I do it anyway, with the rebuke, "Jorge, these things need to be done carefully and properly." It was important to her that we were all serious and meticulous.

Actually, I was used to it. Before I started work at the laboratory, I had spent the whole summer of 1950 as a cleaner at the dyeworks where my father did the books. And from time to time, I did some secretarial work. I used to spend a lot of time at the home of my maternal grandparents, Maria and Francesco, in Calle Quintino Bocayuva. Don Enrico Pozzoli often joined us for lunch. Happy times!

Those years, the 1950s, were in fact the most important in my life: it was in that decade that I experienced work, love, death escaped by a whisker, and a priestly vocation. This last came to me suddenly, on a strange day in early spring.

Between Jorge's studies and the lecture hall, winter has flown by. It is now spring in the Southern Hemisphere. On Monday, September 21, 1953, Buenos Aires woke up to an atmosphere of happy anticipation of this beautiful season. The national student festival, which coincides every year with the arrival of good weather, is in every schoolchild's calendar.

Even though it is not yet eight o'clock in the morning, Jorge is in a hurry to get ready. He wants to wear the suit his mother has pressed for him, because it is a special day: he has arranged to meet friends at the Flores station, where they will be joined by other friends for a celebratory picnic out of town. His father, Mario, left early to take little María Elena to her infant school, but as usual he turned the radio on before setting out. The quality of the programs has gone down a little since the advent of television, which has been broadcasting nationally for some time now, and long-standing announcers have moved on to the new medium. Traditions have not changed in the Bergoglio house, however, not least because Mario loves the classical music broadcasts in the morning and in any case cannot afford this new gadget.

In July, a few weeks before that holiday Monday, the television news, the papers, and the radio had announced the end of the Korean War and then, in September 1953, the election of Nikita Khrushchev as the first secretary of the communist party of the Soviet Union. To many people, having lived through the tumultuous years of Stalinism, this election meant only one thing: the end of the Cold War. To others, however, it is just an interlude: they are certain it will take time to emerge from a logic that divides the world into two power blocs.

Jorge, who thanks to Esther loves reading about politics, follows these developments with interest at home, so that he can discuss them with her and hear what she thinks. In other words, he tries to stay informed as much as possible, so as to understand how the world turns. He also talks with his circle of friends, some of them colleagues at the laboratory. When they meet in the evening to go dancing (tango or rock), or between games of billiards, they talk about communism, Peronism, US capitalism. The Cold War, and its effects on the global economy, is one of their most frequent topics.

But they have other interests too, as is natural. Jorge's stamp collection has become quite substantial; he goes to meetings of Catholic Action in his parish and still enjoys listening to opera and sports on the radio, keeping up to date on San Lorenzo de Almagro. He and his father are true fans. But that early spring morning cannot be wasted listening to the news: his friends are waiting for him at the station.

Reading the papers and listening to the news on the radio, it was very clear that the election of Khrushchev would initiate a thaw in relations between the United States and the Soviet Union, but also that years of rivalry would follow, in technology and industry and, above all, in the space race. A new, Republican president had arrived in the United States, Dwight Eisenhower, and in the Soviet Union the end of Stalin's iron-fist years and the arrival of Khrushchev marked the beginning of a more peaceful period. The two great power blocs had learned how to co-exist and avoid war. In practice they tacitly accepted each other, maintaining their own positions, certain that things would naturally go their way. The important point, during the period leading up to the Cuban missile crisis in 1962, is that it was understood that the use of nuclear weapons would not resolve any differences.

Today, human short-sightedness has paradoxically re-created that Cold War climate. Perhaps some people have forgotten that the world spent decades on edge, peering into the abyss. We escaped only by narrow margins. And yet, even today, we hear the threat of nuclear war being invoked, creating pain and anxiety all over the world.

It is helpful in this context to read again the words of Pope John XXIII: "While it is difficult to believe that anyone would dare to assume responsibility for initiating the appalling slaughter and de-struction that war would bring in its wake, there is no denying that the conflagration could be started by some chance and unforeseen circumstance." Let us not forget that the threat of nuclear weapons makes us all losers: there's no way out.

I remember that September 21, 1953, I had left the house in a hurry. I was due to meet my friends at the station and go on to the student festival. I walked past the Basilica of San José de Flores, which I had been attending since I was a child, and suddenly felt the urge to go in and pay my respects to the Lord. After a prayer said on my knees, I felt a desire to confess. Usually I did this at Almagro, in the Basilica of St. Mary Help of Christians, with some giants of the confessional. I call them giants because they had a unique ability to listen, and were true witnesses of mercy: Father Scandroglio (I was a little afraid of him), Father Montaldo, and Father Punto. At San José that day there was a priest I had never seen before, one Father Carlos Duarte Ibarra, originally from Corrientes. He told me he was in Buenos Aires because he was receiving treatment for serious leukemia. Sadly, he would die the following year.

Something strange happened during that confession, something that truly changed my life: I experienced the shock of unexpectedly meeting God. He was there, waiting for me; He knew I would come. Making confession to that priest, I felt accepted by the Lord's mercy. *"Miserando atque eligendo"* (Looking at Him with mercy and choosing Him), we read in Homily 21 of the English monk Bede the Venerable, a reference to the Gospel story of Jesus inviting Matthew the publican to join and follow him. The office for St. Matthew's Day, September 21, recommends the reading of this meditation. The phrase became my motto when I was a bishop, and now features on the pope's coat of arms. God is the one who always knows we will come: when we sin, He is there, waiting to forgive us, welcome us, grant us His love. And so our faith grows ever deeper. I could say that I "fell to the ground" on that day, as is recounted of Saul of Tarsus, later St. Paul, in the Acts of the Apostles, when he received the Lord's call.

A picnic with friends? Forget it! I was experiencing a particularly wonderful moment in my life—I was putting myself utterly in God's hands! I was overwhelmed. I felt the need to run home and be alone, in silence. And I stayed there for a long time.

Unsurprisingly, I didn't say a word to my family about my call to the priesthood for two years, until I received my diploma and the time came to choose a university. It was 1955, and the only person who knew was Father Duarte, who followed my arduous journey of faith until the day he died. To begin with, I didn't even talk about it with my school friends. There were ten of us in my closest circle, and we referred to ourselves jokingly as the ten *muchachos*. Together we organized evenings in a club in the Chacarita district: we would play billiards, discuss politics, and dance the tango. I loved Juan d'Arienzo's orchestra and, later, the singers Julio Sosa and Ada Falcón, who after a number of love affairs became a nun and went to live in a village in Córdoba.

The moment came to talk to my dad. I plucked up my courage and told him. He was happy with my decision, but I was afraid to tell my mother. I knew she would never accept this choice of mine, so I told her I was going to study medicine. One day, however, while cleaning the house, she found books on theology and philosophy on my desk. She confronted me about my lie and I replied, with a smile, "I really am studying medicine, Mom, the medicine of the soul." She didn't take it well, and Dad had to calm her down, after which she turned to me and said: "I don't know, I don't think it's for you, Jorge. But you're grown up now; try to finish university and then decide." She had obviously dreamed of her firstborn son becoming a doctor.

Grandma Rosa, on the other hand, was very happy. I can still remember her kind words, full of sympathy: "Remember, Jorge, our door is always open. No one will criticize you if you decide to come home one day, but if God is calling you, go: you are blessed."

And so, thanks also to the spiritual guidance of Don Pozzoli, who spent a long time talking to my parents on the occasion of their twentieth wedding anniversary, I made my choice, and at nineteen years of age, accompanied by that admirable Salesian, I entered the archdiocesan seminary in Villa Devoto. I was given responsibility for the youngest seminarians, among them Leonardo Sandri, the twelve-year-old son of immigrants from Trento. I met him again years later in the Vatican, as a cardinal.

During that year at the seminary I experienced a minor lapse. This is normal. We wouldn't be human otherwise. I had been engaged once, to a very sweet girl who worked in the world of cinema and went on to marry and have children. Now, at the wedding of an uncle of mine, I found myself dazzled by a particular young woman. She was so beautiful, so clever, it made my head spin. For a week I kept picturing her in my mind's eye, and found it difficult to pray. Fortunately it passed, and I was able to dedicate my mind and body to my vocation.

Until there came yet another test. It was August 1957. My grandparents were about to celebrate their fiftieth wedding anniversary, but a few days before the day, everyone in the seminary caught the flu. I was infected too, but whereas the other boys recovered and started going out again, I stayed shut up in my room: the fever wouldn't pass. One day my condition got worse: my temperature was very high, and the frightened rector rushed me to the Syrian Lebanese Hospital. I was diagnosed with a serious infection; that day they sucked more than two pints of fluid from my lungs. I was cared for by an Italian nurse to whom I owe my life: Sister Cornelia Caraglio, a Dominican. She realized the dosage of penicillin that had been prescribed for me was insufficient, so she administered the right amount for my condition and saved me. And fellow seminarians with the same blood type came every day to give blood. I had so many guardian angels!

My convalescence was long. I spent a great deal of time in silence. I thought about what might happen to me, I prayed to the Madonna, and to a certain extent I prepared myself for death—which might come suddenly; this could not be ruled out. Indeed, every time my mother came to see me she burst into tears; others tried to comfort me. In November they removed the upper lobe of my right lung, which had developed three cysts. The surgical procedure used the techniques of the day: you can imagine the incisions they made, and how I suffered.

Once out of the hospital, I decided to leave the seminary and join a religious order, the Jesuits: I was very attracted to their missionary vocation, and I liked their discipline. They would admit me in March, but it was still November and the summer was about to begin. Thanks to Don Pozzoli, I spent a month among other young clerics at Villa Don Bosco, a mountain residence in Tandil, surrounded by greenery. Don Pozzoli never tried to get me to join their congregation: he respected my choice and didn't proselytize.

And so, on March 11, 1958, I joined the Society of Jesus. There followed years of study, first in Argentina and at a mission in Chile, then teaching at the College of the Immaculate Conception in Santa Fe and at the College of the Savior in Buenos Aires. By now it was the mid-1960s, and I was officially a *maestrillo*, or trainee, but the students called me *carucha*, or babyface, on account of my youth—I was not yet thirty. Those young people were certainly creative!

I taught literature and psychology in those schools, and some of my pupils were very inquisitive, sometimes even rebellious. On one occasion, a boy called Roberto slapped a smaller boy during a game of football. It was a serious matter, but rather than punishing him I thought up a different lesson. I told him to meet me in a classroom on a particular day at a particular time. When he arrived, he found ten of his classmates sitting in a circle with me. I asked him to tell them all what had happened, and to give his reasons for what he had done. Some of his friends consoled him, others gave him advice, a few laughed the whole thing off (I pretended not to notice). And then this special "student committee" decided on its punishment: an immediate apology to the boy he had slapped and a two-week suspension from all sporting activities. This stratagem of mine had a double aim: on one hand, it was the students themselves, and not the teachers, who punished his bad behavior; on the other hand, the boys experience the meaning of the word *community*.

I remember another pupil at the college in Santa Fe, Jorge Milia. When he grew up he became a lawyer, and today he is a writer and journalist. One day he handed in a literature essay after the deadline, and for this he was held back. He performed brilliantly in a repeat oral exam before a committee made up of me and two brother priests. He deserved ten out of ten, but at my suggestion we gave him nine. I told him, "Your exam is worth ten, but you'll get nine, so you won't forget your years in this college." And I think poor Jorge remembers it to this day! We are still in touch: he moved to Mallorca and occasionally comes to see me in the Vatican.

There was so much enthusiasm among the boys who were planning to go to university. This was when the phenomenon of the Beatles, a rock group I had not heard of at the time, traveled all the way from Europe to our part of the world. It was 1965, and one day a small group of students knocked on my door, wanting to set up a band to copy those performers from Britain. They did not have a space, or the means, to work together as a foursome. They showed me a record with a picture of the group from Liverpool, and when I saw their long hair I joked, "I hope you're not planning on becoming longhairs, like them?" We made a deal: they would study hard, and I would support them. With no little trouble I managed to find them a room to practice once a week, some audio equipment (microphones and loudspeakers) that was normally used by the rector of the college, and a translator—one of our students, who would listen to the Beatles' records and translate the lyrics into Spanish. I encouraged those young men to perform in public in front of their classmates, though these occasions were somewhat jinxed by non-functioning amplification equipment. Unfortunately, they all followed different paths toward university after their fifth-year exams, and the group broke up. It was a wonderful experiment, though, and of course yet another opportunity to build community.

They were all very attentive, the boys, especially during the last two years of high school. In my courses on Spanish and Argentine literature I tried to push them to do some creative writing, and explained that it was necessary to distinguish between what schoolbooks said and what authors wrote. This is why I organized roundtable discussions in class with writers. María Esther Vásquez came once: she had written books with Jorge Luis Borges, and together they had a radio show about literature; later we also hosted Borges himself, and the discussions with him were memorable. I also invited María Esther de Miguel, at that time the young author of a bestseller, *Los que comimos a Solís* (We who ate Solís), which impressed the students greatly with its writing, and also its beauty.

These were very important formative experiences for the students, but also for me: step by step, I was getting ready for my ordination as a priest in 1969.

V

LANDING ON THE MOON

Despite the lateness of the hour, the lights are on all over the Colegio Máximo de San José. This enormous 1930s brick building, surrounded by some ninety acres of greenery, lies about thirty miles northwest of central Buenos Aires and houses Jesuit seminarians, students of philosophy and theology. Tonight they have gathered to watch a special occasion on television.

It is nearly ten p.m. on Sunday, July 20, 1969. It is very cold outside; very few people are out and about this late. Some are enjoying the show in their homes, sitting in armchairs in front of heaters; others are watching in the homes of friends or in the few bars that are still open. The Jesuits' TV lounge is very simple: forty-odd chairs, a crucifix on the white wall, huge green curtains all the way to the floor. In the middle of the room, high up, a medium-size television. All the chairs are occupied: the rector has given the students permission to stay up to watch the historic live broadcast of the moon landing. But the central heating is off, as usual at this hour of the day.

Young Jorge Bergoglio is sitting in that hall too. The television, one of nearly two million in Argentina by now, is tuned to channel 13. The Telenoche *news show has sent Mónica Cahen D'Anvers, its well-known anchor, to NASA's Kennedy Space Center at Cape Canaveral in Florida, where the Saturn V rocket sent the Apollo 11 mission on its way, with the astronauts Neil Armstrong, Edwin "Buzz" Aldrin, and Michael Collins on board. It is a historic moment for the world, and also for Argentina: this live broadcast is the first to arrive via the brand-new satellite station at Balcarce, an isolated settlement in the countryside southeast of the capital.*

The excitement of witnessing this historic moment and being able to say "I was there" has kept everyone up, young and old, till nearly midnight, though by now the thirty-two-year-old Jorge would rather be in his room, getting ready for bed. He will at last be ordained as a priest in less than five months, and he likes to spend his evenings in silence and prayer, preparing himself for this great event. During this preordination period, in fact, in a moment of great spiritual intensity, he has handwritten a profession of faith. Tonight he has letters to answer, some of them from former students at the boarding school in Santa Fe; a book of poetry by Friedrich Hölderlin on the bedside table; notes to revise. And he likes to get up very early in the morning.

But seeing a man set foot on the moon is a once-in-a-lifetime event, which is why all the country's main newspapers have banner headlines on the front page about the moon landing. There is not a sound to be heard, not even the buzzing of a fly, among the seminarians: they are silent, listening to the words of the reporter in the United States and the commentary from the studio in Buenos Aires.

It was a truly unforgettable night! There we all were in the TV lounge, watching those images arrive on the screen from so far

68

away. We really couldn't miss the occasion, particularly as we were lucky enough to have a television at the seminary, which in those days was almost a luxury. Even in black and white, the quality of the images was pretty good. It was remarkable to see Neil Armstrong's footprints in the dust, with the announcer on Argentine TV giving a live translation of the English-language commentary from CBS, the US station in charge of the transmission. And of course there was the moment when the astronaut said the words, transmitted to us in Spanish, that have entered into history: "That's one small step for man, one giant leap for mankind." The excitement!

Some of the boys had already turned on the television by three in the afternoon, when the live broadcast began. It continued well into the small hours, an uninterrupted marathon from the early afternoon on. Suffice it to say that Armstrong set foot on the lunar surface a scant six hours after the landing, when it was nearly midnight in Argentina, and we were all there, holding our breath. Still, I had much to do that day, so I didn't go into the lounge until ten, by which time we were very nearly at the moment of disembarkation. At the moment when Armstrong set foot on the moon and shortly after, when he and his fellow astronaut Buzz Aldrin planted the American flag in the lunar soil, we sat open-mouthed and checked the clock, so as to remember the moment forever. It was so unbelievable!

In Argentina, the days leading up to this event had been marked by a furious row because a satellite fault had prevented us from following the launch of the Apollo 11 mission on July 16. So there was great anticipation that evening, but also a worry that the transmission might be interrupted at the crucial moment.

At the seminary, as elsewhere, there were of course a few kill-joys who said provocative things during the broadcast like, "Don't be taken in. This is all a lie, it was filmed in a studio." We almost got into an argument about what technological progress was and was not capable of achieving. Fortunately, one of our supervisors quickly intervened to silence the ones who were doing the talking: the moment was too important to be ruined. That evening, though, I believe we all understood instinctively that the world would now be different somehow.

Progress is fundamental—we have to keep moving—but it must be in harmony with humankind's ability to manage it. If it is not in harmony, and advances on its own, it turns into something inhuman that cannot be managed. The risk was present back then, and it is still there today—with artificial intelligence, for example, something that is more and more present in our lives but which, if used wrongly or in criminal ways, can be very dangerous. Consider the "fake news," supported by fake evidence, that is skillfully created by these new technological tools. This cannot but stimulate fresh reflection and raise questions that have not previously been considered. We need an ethical approach to these new realities, and in fact I have spoken in the past about algorethics, a new field of study that considers the interaction of human beings and machines, to ensure that they always develop within the parameters of respect for the person.

Watching those images of men on the moon we felt awed, a community united in feeling small in the face of the enormity of what was happening. The same thing happens when we think about space: we are but a tiny droplet in the infinity of the universe. If one tomorrow we discover that there are other forms of life out there, it will only be because God has willed it. The existence and intelligibility of the universe are not the fruit of chaos or chance but of divine wisdom, present, as we read in chapter 8, verse 22, of the book of Proverbs, "at the beginning of his work, the first of his acts of old."

We must always persevere in our search for truth, accept new scientific discoveries with humility, and not repeat the mistakes of the past: by treading a path toward the boundaries of human knowledge it is possible to achieve a true experience of the Lord, who is in a position to fill our hearts.

The principles of the Church's social doctrine are our beacon. They offer a decisive contribution: justice, dignity of the human, subsidiarity, solidarity. Harm follows, though, when new technological or scientific discoveries are bent to other purposes. Consider the use of new technologies in warfare, or the exploitation of new knowledge to create embryos in test tubes and then destroy them, leading to the practice of renting out uteruses, an inhuman practice that is more and more widespread, that threatens the dignity of both men and women and treats children like commodities.

We must always protect human life, from conception to death. I shall never tire of saying that abortion is murder, a criminal act: there is no other word for it. It involves discarding, eliminating a human life that is without fault. It is a defeat for anyone who carries it out and anyone who is complicit in it: mercenaries, killers for hire! No more abortions, please! It is vital that we defend and promote objections of grounds of conscience.

And how can we help women? By being at their side, by being welcoming, so that they don't arrive at the drastic choice of abortion, which is certainly not the solution to their problems. We must make it understood that life is sacred, a gift we have received from God, and it mustn't be thrown away just like that. As long as I have voice, I will shout this out loud. I've been doing so in my addresses and homilies since that far-off year of 1969, the year of my ordination as a priest and man's landing on the moon.

After that historic night, the world talks of nothing else: the moon landing is the topic of the moment. America is celebrating; Armstrong and Aldrin, as well as their colleague Michael Collins, pilot of the conical Apollo 11 command module Columbia, are heroes. Children begin to dream of being like them, and radio and television specials and documentaries explore a range of ideas, including conspiracy theories.

All eyes are now on the return to Earth of the three "spacemen," two of whom spent more than two hours outside their capsule, on lunar soil. Jorge is curious to hear what his family has to say, and the following day he calls his mother and grandmother to ask whether they saw the live transmission. They had indeed watched it on TV: they were still thrilled and could not quite believe it.

These are also the emotions of many of Jorge's friends. The whole adventure is discussed in detail; the rector has posted on the noticeboard a message issued by Pope Paul VI the previous evening from the Vatican Observatory at Castel Gandolfo. The pope, having looked at the moon through the telescope, had watched the live broadcast in the company of Father Daniel O'Connell, director of the observatory. "Here, from his observatory at Castel Gandolfo, near Rome," the pope said, "Pope Paul VI is speaking to you astronauts. Honor, greetings, and blessing to

you, conquerors of the moon, pale lamp of our nights and our dreams!
Bring to her, with your living presence, the voice of the Spirit, a hymn
to God, our Creator and our Father."

In the refectory, over lunch, the talk is of the pontiff's words and the
images seen on the television, not soccer, nor even philosophy or theol-
ogy. Nothing is as interesting as the space race, this American project,
and reactions to it from the Church and the rest of the world, including
the Soviet Union.

"Jorge, would you have traveled to the moon?" his friend Andrés
teases him as he passes over the tortellini in broth.

"Oh no, I'm just fine here! I've got something important coming up
in a few months, you know," Jorge answers with a smile.

"Our very own Jorge is becoming a priest at last. But I wonder where
they'll send you for the third stage of your probation, before your final
vows?" says another student, Francisco.

"Only God knows! Let's talk about the moon now, a much more in-
teresting subject," says Jorge, cutting the conversation short by throw-
ing some water over his interlocutor.

There really was no other topic of conversation. And it went on like
this for months: my preparation for ordination certainly involved
praying at the tabernacle, lived as an experience of complete surrender to the Lord, but also constant discussions about and news from
the new frontier of space opened up by the Americans.

After they returned to Earth, the three astronauts were kept in
quarantine. I remember that when it was over, in mid-August, they
received the Presidential Medal of Freedom from President Richard

Nixon. They were then feted in New York, Chicago, and Los Angeles with parades in the streets. In mid-October 1969, they went to the Vatican and were received by the pope. Paul VI's words on that day made an impression on me. Addressing the three astronauts, he said man has a natural tendency to explore the unknown, to understand its mystery; but he also has a fear of it. He went on to tell them that their bravery had transcended that fear, allowing man to take another step toward knowing more about the universe.

I must admit that I too may have been subconsciously feeling a bit of fear at that time, because something significant awaited me, the priesthood. I didn't know what would happen afterward, and I was apprehensive. It's only human. And so, with those words of Paul VI impressed on my mind, I did a great deal of reflecting on the subject of fear. I thought about Jesus, who always told his followers not to be afraid. If we are with God and love our brothers and sisters, it is love that will triumph, the love that casts out fear, as we read in the Gospel of John.

Consider the great religions: they do not teach fear and division. They teach harmony, unity, tolerance. Fear, on the other hand, paralyzes human relationships, threatens faith, feeds suspicion of the other, of the unknown, of the different. Some might counter, "I can't help it. I'm afraid, it's stronger than me." At which point it is necessary to ask for the gift of the Holy Spirit, which frees us from fear and opens up our hearts. It gives us the strength to face the hardest situations, even the ones we don't know about. A small amount is enough, and it feels good, because if we remain slaves to fear, we will find ourselves blocked, in the expectation that something terrible will happen.

And then, accompanied by prayers and thanks to the Lord for the gift I was to receive, the day of my ordination arrived at last: it was December 13, 1969, four days before my thirty-third birthday. My brothers and sisters attended mass at the college, as did my mother, who knelt before me afterward and asked for my blessing, and Grandma Rosa, who looked at me with eyes full of love and joy. My father, sadly, had died by then: he passed away in 1961 after three heart attacks, the first while he was at the stadium with my brother Alberto, the other two in the days that followed. Also absent was Don Pozzoli: unfortunately we had lost him the same year as my dad. Two huge losses in the same year.

As for Grandma Rosa, she had been convinced she would never live to see the day and had therefore written me a very beautiful letter two years earlier, in 1967. She wrote partly in Italian and partly in Spanish, leaving instructions to give me the letter on the day of my ordination, along with her gift, a chest containing everything necessary for the Sacrament of the Anointing of the Sick. But she was able to attend my ordination after all. Very much so! I have carefully preserved that short letter ever since, along with her testament of faith and a poem by Nino Costa, "*Rassa nostrana*" (Our race), among the pages of my breviary.

Rosa wrote: "This wonderful day, on which you can hold Christ the Savior in your sanctified hands and the long journey toward a deeper apostolate lies open to you, I give you this modest gift, of scant material value but of great spiritual value."

My grandmother died five years later, in 1974, bequeathing to her grandchildren some wonderful words, which I often read at difficult moments, even now when I am pope: "If one day they should be afflicted with pain, illness, or the loss of a loved one, let them remember that a breath at the tabernacle wherein is kept the greatest and most noble martyr of all, and a glance at Mary at the foot of the cross, will cause a drop of balsam to fall on the deepest and most painful of wounds."

She really was a great woman. Her heart, like that of many old people, was for me a spring from which gushed the living water of the faith that quenched my thirst. She passed on the gospel by means of tenderness, attention, wisdom. Faith is born like this. It is passed on in a gentle song in dialect, in a climate of family, in the mother tongue. Grandparents are a precious source: we must care for them and protect them, not park them in a care home. They must not be treated as something to be discarded; they must not be considered a burden. We owe them everything: they have helped us grow, they have given us the bread from their own mouths, they have made us what we are, constantly encouraging and supporting us.

And yet it can happen in the best families that, when an aging grandparent becomes a nuisance or complains too much, he or she is sent straight to a care home and abandoned there. But, forgotten and discarded as they may be, I'm certain they continue to pray for their children and grandchildren. They remain at our sides even when they're no longer with us. I too feel my grandmother near me at the most difficult times, as I felt her during the most difficult times for Argentina, the dark days of dictatorship.

VI

THE VIDELA COUP
IN ARGENTINA

A group of young priests in shirtsleeves has been walking in and out of the college for more than an hour. They are carrying large boxes, furniture, files, books, and a number of sacred objects used till now in the Jesuits' provincial curia. It is very hot. It is March 24, 1976, and autumn has officially just begun. On the streets of the San Miguel district of Buenos Aires, everyday life is going on as usual, but that life has fallen silent because, over the past year or so, people have become accustomed to an atmosphere of suspicion and sudden violence affecting many parts of society.

The seeds of terror were sown by extreme right-wing paramilitary groups close to certain members of the government of Isabel Perón. Priests and bishops working closely with the poor have already been targeted, suspected of subversion. But anyone who supports the communist ideology, whether actively or not, has a target on their back.

Father Jorge Bergoglio, now thirty-nine years old, has been the provincial superior, leader of the Society of Jesus in Argentina, for the previous three years. He has an extremely heavy box of documents in his hands. *Together with a willing group of priests, he is completing the curia's move to the Colegio Máximo de San José in San Miguel, where Jorge studied, would begin to teach, and would eventually become rector. His decision to transfer the Jesuit headquarters to this place is based on a desire to balance the books in the face of a rising number of calls to the priesthood: these are increasing every year, and Bergoglio believes that even he, the provincial superior, must stay in close contact with both the trainers and the future members of the society.*

The small band of Jesuits, preoccupied as they are with the movement of boxes from the van to the interior of the college, is unaware of what is going on in the heart of Buenos Aires at that very moment: the armed forces have deposed the Perón government, and a military junta with neoliberal ideas has seized power. General Jorge Rafael Videla leads the coup and is soon sworn in as president of Argentina, alongside the head of the navy, Admiral Emilio Massera, and the head of the air force, General Orlando Ramón Agosti. Chaos follows: the constitution is suspended, parliament is dissolved, martial law is declared. Radio and television stations are occupied, armored vehicles fan out on the streets. Anyone even suspected of being a leftist subversive, or linked to populist circles or nonaligned trade unions, is abducted and tortured in secret by the military. Soldiers travel through the streets in green cars with no plates: the notorious Ford Falcons.

Tens of thousands of people disappear under the regime, the desaparecidos (the disappeared). Most of them are young people, murdered after months of torture; many are tossed out of helicopters or military aircraft, sometimes drugged, and swallowed alive by the ocean. These are the so-called death flights. Meanwhile, their children

are kidnapped and handed over to regime-friendly families. Many peo-
ple are forced to leave the country, and political prisoners are executed.
This is the so-called dirty war.

A few military patrols appear at San Miguel that hot autumn
day and drive around the Jesuit college. Father Jorge is not at all sur-
prised to see them buzzing about in the area: he knows that priests
are watched because many curas villeros, priests who work in the
slums, are considered to be communist sympathizers and therefore a
threat to the national reorganization process. The soldiers observe a
suspicious movement of boxes from the van to the college and decide
to approach.

We were in the process of moving the provincial curia to the Colegio
Máximo, perfectly calmly, with no idea that at that very moment
the government was being overturned by the military in a coup that
would change the face of Argentina. The soldiers, seeing all those
boxes, came over and started asking questions. They wanted to
know what we were doing, why we were there, what was in the boxes,
and so on.

At first perhaps they thought we were getting ready to escape, or
maybe that we were getting rid of compromising material, given the
news of the change of government. But we really didn't know anything; we were just quietly going about our business. I explained to
the commander of the patrol that it was a simple office move. After
a few minutes, they were convinced and left, fortunately. These were
not simple times. Risk was always just around the corner, although
we knew very well that certain elements of the Church were being

persecuted while others—the ones that had fallen in line with the regime—enjoyed complete freedom.

I understood this problem clearly when I met Monsignor Enrique Angelelli, bishop of La Rioja, in 1973. In La Rioja, more than six hundred miles from the capital, the persecution of the church of the streets had been much more vicious than what we faced in our area. This sainted priest lived for the poor, and for the *campesinos* (peasants) exploited by the owners of the largest estates, the *latifundistas*. He was later targeted by the military because of his service among the exploited, and because he campaigned alongside them—all within the guidelines of the Second Vatican Council.

Monsignor Angelelli, like Monsignor Óscar Romero, the archbishop of San Salvador who was murdered in 1980 while celebrating mass in a hospital chapel, was accused of preaching a Marxist interpretation of the gospel, thus embracing the liberation theology that was inspired by left-wing political ideology. This is not true! The choice made by these Latin American priests, like many priests in the Global South, was based on the Vatican Council's revision of the schema of the Church to define its adherents as "people of God." This idea was later reinforced during the Second Episcopal Conference of Latin America, held in Medellín, Colombia, in 1968, which described a Church that chooses to care for the poor and rallies around the lower strata of society, affirming their history and culture; a Church that preaches the gospel with a Christian perspective, rather than one based on politics.

Angelelli's work with the poor was considered subversive, however, and he too ended up in the sights of the dictatorship, which automatically labeled as communist anyone who worked with these social groups. The bishop knew they wanted to destroy him and those around him, so in 1975, when he learned that the secret services were closing in on him, he asked me to hide three of his seminarians in the Colegio Máximo. I kept them at the college for quite a while, under the pretext of spiritual exercises.

Angelelli had informed the papal nuncio in Argentina, Monsignor Pio Laghi, of death threats he had received, but was killed on August 4, 1976, while driving his truck in the company of another priest, Arturo Pinto. The vehicle was rammed and forced into a ravine. Pinto was left for dead, but survived. The case was filed as a road accident that same day, and what upset me was that the archbishop of Buenos Aires, Cardinal Juan Carlos Aramburu, accepted the regime's version. But these were difficult times for the Church. The individuals who ordered the assassination, two ex-soldiers collaborating with the regime, weren't identified and given life sentences until July 2014.

Those three seminarians from La Rioja assisted me in welcoming other young men at risk, at least twenty of them in two years, whom we passed off as students taking courses in religion or participants in spiritual retreats. But they were terrible years, with many difficult situations to resolve. For example, I believed the secret services had me under surveillance, so I found ways to send them off on the wrong track when I spoke on the telephone or wrote letters. I asked the young Jesuits in the college not to go out after dark and never alone, only in groups, so that it would be more difficult to abduct them. And I also forbade them to discuss politics if they found themselves talking to other priests, especially military chaplains, in the refectory or during breaks. Not everyone was loyal to the Church, and I think a few such existed within our college. Unsurprisingly, there were night searches in the novices' residence, Villa Barilari, but we got through them without problems.

During that time I was presented with the case of a young man who needed to escape from Argentina. I noticed that he looked like me, so I managed to get him out dressed as a priest and equipped with my identity card. This time I was taking a big risk: if he had been found out, the authorities would undoubtedly have killed him and then come looking for me.

I also remember the story of Sergio and Ana, a couple who lived with their daughter as lay teachers among the poor. I had met them before I became a priest, and used to go and visit them often. They were a very Catholic family, in no way communist or subversive, but they were falsely denounced by the secret police. Sergio was taken away without warning and tortured for days. I tried everything to free him, and in the end I succeeded, thanks to the intervention of the Italian consul, Enrico Calamai, a great man who saved many people.

I must admit that I too was the victim of smears during the years of the dictatorship: I was accused of handing over to the regime two Jesuits who worked in a Bajo Flores slum, Father Orlando Yorio and Father Franz Jalics. These two priests were building a religious congregation of their own, and in my capacity of provincial superior I warned them, in the name of the superior general, that this would result in their dismissal from the Society of Jesus—which duly took place a year later.

In addition, I advised them to leave the slum temporarily, because there had been hints that the military might carry out a lightning raid and take them away. I offered them hospitality in the college, if necessary, but they decided to remain with the poor, and in May 1976, they were abducted. I did everything in my power to get them freed. I spoke to Admiral Massera twice, because it was said that the pair had been taken by navy men. I also managed to speak to General Videla once, after arranging by subterfuge to celebrate mass in his home one Saturday afternoon. The following day, I referred the whole matter to Father Pedro Arrupe, the superior general, who lived in Rome: I called him from a public telephone in Avenida Corrientes.

The street is particularly crowded on a Sunday morning. Despite the road blocks and the green cars of the federal police speeding past all the time, families are trying to enjoy the respite of a day off. The air is filled with the constant fear of being suddenly seized by a passing patrol, of being searched in the street, back to the wall, or, worse, being beaten up.

Father Jorge says mass in the college very early, and then leaves discreetly. He takes the bus to Avenida Corrientes, a main street in central Buenos Aires, where he uses a payphone to make sensitive phone calls. He does not want his conversations to be overheard, and he fears the telephones in the curia are bugged. On the bus, he recites his rosary and finds himself listening to the other passengers' whispered conversations: mothers weeping over the disappearance of their children and young people who would like to protest against the cruelty of the regime.

The Jesuit loses himself in prayer. Because his eyes are closed, he nearly misses his stop; he is thinking about the two priests in the hands of the military when the driver, luckily, announces it.

Father Jorge looks around: a car fitted with loudspeakers gives advice to citizens on how to behave if stopped by the police; patrols stroll down the sidewalk, glancing into shops; meanwhile, the regime's plain-clothes men are in the churches, sitting at the back and listening to the priests' homilies.

Father Jorge inserts some tokens and dials the number. "Father General, it's Bergoglio."

"Jorge, it's a pleasure to hear your voice. What news?"

"I managed to meet with Videla yesterday," the young provincial superior whispers, afraid a patrol might overhear him.

"How did you manage that?" Father Pedro Arrupe asks, intrigued.

"I persuaded the military chaplain who usually says mass at his home to call in sick, and then I took his place. I showed up and celebrated mass at his residence. After mass I spoke to him. Videla told me he would intervene to resolve the matter. Let's hope he really will."

From that payphone, far from the curia, Father Jorge updates the superior general every time there is news of the fate of those two priests. But one day, five months after their abduction, it is Father Jorge who receives an unexpected call at the college.

It is Father Yorio himself, tearfully announcing that he has been freed: he and Father Jalics had been drugged and then dumped in a field in Cañuelas, an hour's drive from Buenos Aires. After months of violence and humiliation, the two priests are free at last. Through the good offices of the papal nunciature, Father Jorge is able to get diplomatic cover for them and organizes their departure from the country:

Jalics joins his mother in the United States, while Yorio is sent to Rome to study canon law.

As the months go by, Father Jorge pays close attention to the cases of other desaparecidos, keeping an open channel to the papal nuncio, but he also has to keep up with other, less vital but nevertheless important matters. For example, the children in the neighborhoods around the college receive no pastoral care and minimal education, so on Saturday afternoons he organizes catechism and the occasional game of soccer. This closeness to the youngsters earns him the charge, from within the Society of Jesus, of having "Salesianized" the society's education.

Obviously he must also consider his priests, their spiritual and bodily health. Sunday is the cook's day off, and it is the provincial superior himself who makes both lunch and supper for the students. He learned to cook from Grandma Rosa and his mother: after the birth of María Elena, his mother asked her older children to help at mealtimes and made sure all the ingredients were ready and on the table for them.

Jorge also received a few culinary tips from Esther, and one day she got in touch with her former laboratory assistant.

Despite our different commitments, Esther and I saw each other often during those years. I used to visit her at home when I could, for dinner or afternoon coffee. I was still fond of her. After all, she taught me to think. I stayed close to her during her darkest hours. In September 1976, the military seized her son-in-law, and then, the next year, they took her daughter Ana María, too, sixteen years old and pregnant. The whole family was under surveillance because the regime was very familiar with this communist woman's history and political engagement.

That day her telephone call was really odd; in a different voice from her usual she said, "Listen Jorge, my mother-in-law, Edelmira, is close to the end. Can you come and give her the last rites?" Something wasn't right. Although Esther's mother-in-law was a believer, she and her family were atheists. I sensed there was something else, something my friend couldn't tell me over the telephone. So I went to her home, bringing the anointing kit my grandmother had given me just in case. I knocked and Esther opened the door, quickly closing it behind me in case I had been followed.

I played it safe. "What's going on, Esther?" She explained everything immediately. "I'm being watched, Jorge. I'm under surveillance. If they come in and find all these books, I'm finished." To cut a long story short, she asked me to hide all the books: there were several books on Marxist thought, volumes of philosophy, and other texts that, if found by the regime, would be destroyed. In the days that followed I got organized: I took them away and held them in the college library, mixed up with all the others.

Ana María was released after four months in prison, and Esther decided to take her and her two older daughters to Sweden, where many Argentines had sought refuge. One of the sisters still lives there, while the other two eventually returned to Argentina. I saw them a few years ago.

Having taken the girls to safety, Esther came back to Argentina: she was one of the few Mothers of the Plaza de Mayo to continue in the movement even after getting their children back. She was still worried, though, and rightly so. She joined the group of protestors in the square every Thursday afternoon, all of them wearing their trademark white kerchiefs on their heads; but the group had been infiltrated, on the orders of Admiral Massera, by a young naval officer with the face of an angel, Alfredo Astiz. He had introduced himself with a fake name, Gustavo, and claimed to be the brother of a *desaparecido*. He quickly gained the trust of the group that gathered in the Church of Santa Cruz: he listened to what they said, and gained access to their secrets.

In December 1977, on a day arranged in advance with the police, Astiz gave a signal and the regime's men came to take away some of the women as they emerged from the church after a protest meeting. They took Esther and another of the group's founders, as well as two French nuns, Alice Domon and Léonie Duquet. From what I have learned since, my friend was tortured and then tossed out of an airplane. What a horrible end!

I was able to achieve something for other young people who had been abducted, to make myself useful; but for Esther, her friend, and the two nuns I achieved nothing, despite raising the matter repeatedly with people who could certainly have intervened. Perhaps I didn't do enough for them.

It wasn't until 2005 that her remains were identified, thanks to DNA tests, along with those of María Ponce de Bianco, a founder of the Mothers of the Plaza de Mayo. I was bishop of Buenos Aires at the time, and I authorized their burial in the graveyard of the church from which they had been taken. It was the least I could do.

Nevertheless, the allegations against me continued until a short while ago, revenge on the part of leftists who knew perfectly well how opposed I was to atrocities like this. In the end, thanks partly to the work of a few journalists, witnesses who had stayed silent until then, decided to tell the truth, and the allegations lost their force.

On November 8, 2010, as a person familiar with the facts, I was questioned about crimes committed during the years of dictatorship. There were still people trying to accuse me of collaboration with the junta. The session was held at the archdiocese and lasted four hours and ten minutes. I was subjected to a barrage of questions from lawyers for human rights associations and victims' relatives. There were three judges: the chair, who was very calm; one who said nothing throughout; and another, who attacked me. They even brought up the conclave of 2005, after the death of John Paul II, dredging up the theory that someone in the Vatican had passed around files raising suspicions about my behavior under Videla's regime, with the aim of smearing my reputation and blocking my election. All made up: there weren't any files on me, nor on other cardinal electors.

My cross-examination was recorded, and at the end they told me there was no evidence against me and I was innocent. I met one of the judges twice in the Vatican: the first time he was with some other people, but it was so long since I had seen him in the courtroom that I didn't recognize him; the second time he asked for an audience, and I willingly granted it. Many people have since told me privately that the Argentine government of the day had done its best to put a noose around my neck, but had found no evidence because I was clean.

I prayed to the Lord so hard during those years. Most of all I prayed that He might give peace to those who were personally experiencing violence and humiliation. There is something diabolical about dictatorship: I have seen it with my own eyes, I have lived through moments of great distress, in the fear that something could happen to my younger colleagues. It was a generational genocide.

Fortunately, the nightmare came to an end in the early 1980s, and with the democratic elections in October 1983, things changed for Argentina. They changed for me too: after my experience as provincial superior, I returned as rector of the Colegio Máximo and parish priest of San Miguel in 1980—until I was transferred to Germany in 1986 to study.

VII

THE HAND OF GOD

"Maradona! Maradona! Maradona's unbelievable goal gives Argentina a 1-0 lead over England in the fifty-first minute of this quarter-final. But England are protesting to the referee: they're pointing to their hands. But the goal is given. We have to wait for the replay to see what happened. Let's see: it certainly looks as if he punched it into the goal with his fist and not his head, and Maradona is celebrating with his fist in the air. Incredible!"

The cheers can be heard from the television in the living room. In the street outside the window, silence: no explosion of joy, no celebration. Maximum indifference. West Germans had their fill of excitement the day before, when their team beat Mexico, the hosts, on penalties in their own quarter-final and knocked them out of the World Cup.

One of the few televisions tuned to the match that featured Maradona's goal is that of the Schmidts, the German family hosting Father Jorge in Boppard, a small town an hour's drive from the capital, Bonn. Now forty-nine years old, Jorge has been sent here to improve his German and research material to support the doctoral thesis he is writing on the German-Italian theologian Romano Guardini.

It is June 22, 1986. Father Jorge, a true football fan, would never have chosen to miss this match featuring the pibe de oro, the golden boy. In his number-ten shirt, alongside Jorge Burruchaga and Jorge Valdano, Diego Maradona is giving millions of Argentines a reason to dream; but thanks to a number of unexpected engagements, the Jesuit priest is forced to sit in front of his books, far from the television. The two doctors who are his hosts, however, are watching the match even though it is dinner time and they are at the table. Like many other Germans, they do not seem very interested in this particular match, which is causing such heightened emotion elsewhere. They have tuned in only because they like their guest and want to be able to tell him how it turns out.

After the captain's first goal, the match continues and everyone holds their breath, but the tension lasts only a few minutes: in the fifty-fifth minute, after eluding several England players in a darting, lightning-fast run from within his own half, Maradona scores the goal that goes down in history as the goal of the century. Two-nil to Argentina. A place in the semi-final is getting closer. This time Dr. Schmidt claps with pleasure, a smile on his face as he thinks of Father Jorge.

The cheering continues in the stands of the Aztec Stadium in Mexico City: there are more than one hundred thousand spectators, but it is the whistling of the England fans, who feel cheated by the first goal, illegal in their eyes, that is most audible. Tension between the two teams was already high before they came onto the pitch: their historical rivalry was aggravated by the open wound of the 1982 war that followed Argentina's invasion of the Falkland Islands (Islas Malvinas). And then *the English were further discomfited by a dose of cold water in the form of Maradona, six minutes into the second half.*

At the end of the match, naturally, the champion is in the spotlight again: he kisses his shirt in front of the TV cameras and later, surrounded by microphones, comments that the disputed goal was scored "un poco con la cabeza de Maradona y otro poco con la mano de Dios" *—a little with the head of Maradona, and a little with the hand of God.*

For the first few seconds, no one realized the goal might be illegal, but the English players immediately started protesting to the referee, saying Maradona had struck the ball with his hand. Then, seeing the replay, everyone could see he had used his fist, not his head. The Tunisian referee had not seen it and therefore awarded the goal.

The arguments raged for days: people in Argentina told me the papers discussed the goal endlessly, but front pages all over the world carried the photo, along with the champion's post-match words. When, as pope, I received Maradona in the Vatican a few years ago, we talked of many things, including peace, and then, before he left, I asked him, jokingly, "So, which is the guilty hand?"

I must say that on the field Maradona was a great poet. He scored goals that were destined to go down in history, like the second one in that match, dubbed the goal of the century. His confidence over the ball, however, concealed great fragility in his day-to-day life. We saw this in his last years, with all the problems he had and the pain he caused his fans in Argentina—and also in

Italy, where they know and love him for his triumphant period playing with Napoli.

I watched every game of the 1986 World Cup I could; only when I was busy with something else, or deliberately staying away from the television, did I miss one. At the time I was studying at the Goethe-Institut in Boppard, a small town of fifteen thousand inhabitants. We students were given the opportunity to live with families that offered us hospitality. Among these was a pair of doctors, the Schmidts—she was a homeopath, he a traditional doctor—who lived alone now that their children had grown up and married. Helma Schmidt and her husband wanted company rather than money. Moreover, they were good Catholics: she came and celebrated mass with me in my room every afternoon. Every now and again they would invite me to supper, and we talked about everything from current affairs to sports. This was a good time, and I remember it with great affection.

On the day of the final, June 29, with Argentina facing West Germany, I deliberately chose not to watch the match. Instead, I went for a walk along the Rhine, not far from that kind couple's home. I wanted to carve out a little time for myself, to reflect on my life, to say my rosary, and, as I did every evening, to thank God for everything He had given me, now that I was coming up to fifty years of age.

When I got home, Dr. Schmidt said to me, with a hint of bitterness (he strongly supported West Germany), "It seems you really will be the champions." We were 2-0 up. I thanked him for the news and went to bed without waiting to see how the match ended. He was right: the following morning, still half asleep, I read in the paper that Argentina had won the World Cup 3–2 and that Maradona had lifted the cup himself, as his teammates hoisted him up on their shoulders.

Shortly afterward, as I arrived at the institute, a Japanese fellow student from Sapporo saw me and made a big fuss: "You are the champions! You are the champions!" she said in front of all the others. But the rest of the class remained tight-lipped. There were some English students, and I can understand their reaction, but there were also many French and Italian students. The Japanese student then went up to the blackboard and wrote *VIVA ARGENTINA!* in chalk. I was very happy, but I knew the teacher would be arriving soon, a fine educator who gave me a lot, but a woman who boasted of having been married three times and having children all over the place; perhaps she thought herself very modern! As soon as she saw the writing on the board, she gave the order, "Rub that out!" It seemed that etiquette was to be respected, no matter the circumstances, in that prestigious German institution. Perhaps that was another reason my fellow students didn't say anything to me. I like to think that was the reason, but I felt truly alone at such times, almost an outsider. I had been sent to a place I didn't know and felt so homesick for Argentina.

Even though I couldn't fully share everyone's joy, it was very exciting: we were the world champions! I was reminded of the Argentine championship of 1946, an extraordinary season that was won by our own San Lorenzo. I was a child then, but I still remember our golden trio lifting the cup. We felt tremendous! As often happens, fans hurled insults at the referee during the matches, but so did some of the players, accusing him of being corrupt. At the end of the match, though, they would all shake hands and go back to being friends. That must be the point of sports: competition first, but let it be clean and honest, then have the nobility to embrace one another. That's something the Salesians taught me.

Let us not forget, too, that sports elevate, even when played in the street with a ball in tatters, as I did when I was a little boy. We must ensure that the sporting spirit develops along those lines, the simplest and healthiest lines. I am reminded of a 1948 film called *Pelota de trapo*, or Ragged Ball, by the director Leopoldo Torres Ríos, a pioneer of Argentine cinema. I saw it when I was a teenager. It tells the story of a group of children who play soccer in the street and enjoy what they have, though they dream of one day having a real leather ball. The founder of the Salesians, St. John "Don" Bosco, used to say that if you want to bring children together, all you have to do is place a ball in the street, even if it's made of rags: the youngsters will come running!

In fact, sports, even of the simplest variety, can prevent people from losing their way and lift them up out of troubled families; particularly in urban areas, sports can give young people in difficult circumstances a safety valve that helps them overcome tension by sending them outside for a good kickabout. Salesian priests, too, are born to do this: to save young people from the streets and give them an alternative to the kinds of delinquency they may encounter there. It is a blessing to be able to play sports in this way, as honest fun, because they are a noble cause. Sports need to be accessible to everyone. This is why I am always glad when people get excited about a match, a goal, a win—as long as the amateur dimension, the love of the game for its own sake, is not lost. Sports must be played with passion, for fun; they must be experienced as games. It is true that nowadays there are more commercial aspects to competitive and professional sports, such as sponsors, but this is not a bad thing if done in moderation and ethically. What is important is that the perverse logic of money, which has nothing to do with the spirit of sports, should not take precedence.

The German lesson ended earlier than usual: the teacher had a schedule conflict and left after apologizing to the students and promising to make up the time the next day. Father Jorge, too, decides to take advantage of the extra thirty minutes and say his rosary by the river, where he went the previous evening, rather than go home, where Helma is waiting to celebrate their usual afternoon mass.

Although many citizens are disappointed by their country's second place and have taken down their decorations, there are still a few German flags on balconies and in windows—remnants of that World Cup feeling. Some will be taken to Bonn, where fans are gathering to welcome the national team back from Mexico. Rosettes, trumpets, and replica shirts are already disappearing from shop windows. The disappointment is real: the World Cup was within reach. But in that small provincial town life goes on.

Two very blond boys are out for a walk with their mother. Both have their hair tied up in ponytails—it is very fashionable, especially for the very young—and are wearing replica Germany shirts. They are playing with a small yellow sponge ball, and on their arms they sport drawings of the German flag, done by their father before the final. "I'm Rummenigge," says the older one, "and you're Matthäus, okay?" he adds, tapping his brother on the shoulder.

"And me, an Argentine, who can I be?" asks Father Jorge with a smile, hearing the child fantasizing about his footballing idols. The boys are taken aback: the older one sticks his tongue out, the younger one follows suit. The mother, a little embarrassed, is forced to apologize to this priest she has met by chance.

"Don't worry, ma'am. It means they're proud of their country. And maybe they'll be great footballers when they grow up!" Father Jorge replies fondly, giving a small image of a saint to each child and then going on his way.

On the riverfront, halfway down a row of tables swarming with tourists and residents enjoying the peace of a breezy afternoon, he spots a public telephone. He would like to call his sister María Elena, but he knows she will not be home at this hour. Then he thinks of his friends in Buenos Aires, who are sure to be celebrating the World Cup win.

He checks his plastic watch before approaching: he does not want to be late for his rendezvous with Helma. He knows she and her husband play the piano together before supper, and a delay might prevent that. Fortunately he has a few minutes for a brief call.

He picks up the receiver, inserts the phone card he bought at a kiosk, and calls his old friend Oscar. They have remained close since his laboratory days.

"How are you? Did you watch the final yesterday?" Jorge asks, wasting no time with small talk.

"Everyone's gone mad here, you know. My god, I didn't get a wink of sleep last night! They were celebrating with airhorns, fireworks, firecrackers," says his friend, describing events in Buenos Aires the previous night.

"They're happy, eh?" Jorge says.

"I'll say! But Maradona was in a bit of trouble at the end of the game, because of his 'hand of God.' Lucky he didn't react like the Rat, do you remember?" Oscar asks.

And an old memory is awakened in Jorge, from years ago, when he was not yet thirty.

"The Rat" was the nickname of Antonio Rattín, a great footballer and member of the Argentine national team.

I have a clear memory of a World Cup match played on July 23, 1966, at Wembley Stadium: Argentina were playing the hosts, England, in a quarter-final. It was a match marked by moments of high emotion. Rattín, who was the captain and wore the number-ten shirt, was given a warning by the German referee for a minor foul. This annoyed Rattín. Then the referee gave another member of the Argentine team a warning, and Rattín protested vigorously in Spanish. The referee didn't seem to understand his words, but saw his agitation and gestured to Rattín to leave the field: he had sent him off. Chaos ensued: we, the fans, did not accept the decision.

The Rat refused to leave. He wanted to know why he was being sent off, but there was no interpreter to explain the situation, so play was halted for more than ten minutes. A few officials in jackets and ties came onto the pitch and tried to carry Rattín off, but they failed. When he was finally persuaded to leave, he was met with whistles from the English fans because he did two things on his way back to the changing room that annoyed them: he walked on the red carpet beneath the royal box, which was reserved for the queen, and then he crumpled up a corner flag with the royal crest on it.

Emotion had taken over, and what should have been a moment of pure, clean pleasure had turned into something else. With Maradona in 1986, fortunately, things went differently. But it's not necessary to go very far back to find other unpleasant moments. In the most recent World Cup, in Qatar in 2022, for example, I read that French fans whistled at the Argentine goalkeeper, Emiliano Martínez, at the end of the final, and he replied with an offensive gesture. And then there was the on-field fracas during the Argentina–Netherlands quarter-final. I hated this, because the end of a match should be a celebration for everyone, without disputes, the losers being consoled and the winners embraced. The spirit of sport should prevail, not resentment.

I didn't watch the last World Cup because I don't watch television anymore—I'll explain why later—but on the day of the final, during the game against France, I was with four airline pilots, friends of friends who had come to see me with their wives. One of them said to me, "Argentina's 2-0 up. The cup is yours!" In the end, I learned, Argentina won on penalties, and not without pain, because the French were tough. This made me think: in the quarter-finals, for example, Argentina was 2-0 up against the Netherlands, but the match ended with penalties. It was the same story in the final: winning to begin with, but then caught up with at the end.

Maybe this way of doing things is part of the psychology of certain Argentines. At first they are enthusiastic, and then, lacking tenacity, they struggle to reach the end. We Argentines are like that: we think we have victory in hand, and then, in the second half, we risk losing. And it's not only in football that we lack tenacity, it's also in everyday life. Before we bring something to its conclusion, we indulge ourselves a little too much and perhaps don't achieve the result we hoped for. Fortunately, though, in the end we manage to get through.

Back to Germany in 1986, and my mind pauses to remember something that goes beyond victory in the World Cup and Maradona's handball goal: In that country I experienced to the full my devotion to the Madonna who unties all knots. While still in Buenos Aires, I had heard about a painting called *Maria Knotenlöserin* (Mary, Untier of Knots). As the name suggests, it depicts the Virgin, surrounded by angels, untying knots. It is kept in the ancient Jesuit church of St. Peter am Perlach in Augsburg, Bavaria, but unfortunately I have never been there. If my commitments had allowed it, I would have liked to pray before this eighteenth-century Baroque painting, thinking about all the knots I needed to untie. I was on a sabbatical approved by my provincial, but there was still no shortage of disputes, difficulties, sins, and seemingly insurmountable obstacles to be confronted during this period of my life.

And this was when, despite everything, I once again felt the presence of the Lord, who was ready for me, and the Madonna. She stood by the gate to my heart, listening to my complaints with the patience only a mother can have. Not only that: I entrusted myself entirely to her, and I felt she was helping me untie my knots. And this doesn't apply only to me, it applies to everyone. Marian devotion must be like this: clear, beautiful, clean, simple. Mary and her son Jesus must be always in the foreground, without intermediaries to exploit and profit from people's innocence and weakness.

One day I found a quantity of picture cards showing this painting, and I took them back to Buenos Aires with me when my time in

Germany came to an end. I gave them as gifts as I circulated among friends, acquaintances, and the faithful. Several reproductions of *Mary, Untier of Knots*, have been made over the years. Some of them can still be found in churches in Buenos Aires, where this particular Marian cult has grown stronger, attracting more and more of the faithful.

Meanwhile, having returned to my home country, I took up my day-to-day life again, starting at the Colegio del Salvador in Buenos Aires.

VIII

THE FALL OF
THE BERLIN WALL

The room, small and austere, with no private bathroom, is filled with the melodies of Wagner: *Parsifal*, under the baton of maestro Hans Knappertsbusch, accompanies Father Jorge during his afternoon's work at the Colegio del Salvador, the prestigious Jesuit elementary and secondary school in the congested heart of Buenos Aires.

For Father Jorge this is a return, for he taught literature and philosophy here in 1966. After his brief residence in Germany, here he is again in this Jesuit community, this time as confessor in the nearby church of Salvador. The new provincial superior, Father Víctor Zorzín, who was Jorge's deputy from 1973 to 1979 when Jorge was Jesuit provincial of Argentina and Uruguay, has decided to give him this minor post, which entails no responsibilities to the governance of the Society of Jesus, and Father Jorge has obeyed.

His contributions to the Argentine Jesuit theological journal Stromata have made Father Jorge Bergoglio well known among his fellow priests in Argentina, and the late 1980s are therefore a period of intense activity for him. He writes articles, gives lectures all over Argentina, leads spiritual retreats; most significant of all, he has been invited by Father Ernesto López Rosas, a prominent exponent of teología del pueblo, or people's theology, and the new rector of the Colegio Máximo at San Miguel, to give a weekly class in pastoral theology to the college's students, who are already using Bergoglio's works in their studies. Father López has known him since the late 1960s. They have held the same views on pastoral care, social commitment on the part of the clergy, and a focus on the working class since they used to gather around the Jesuit Miguel Ángel Fiorito, a spiritual guide for many of his fellow Argentine clerics.

Father Jorge, immersed in the works of Romano Guardini and St. Augustine, with Parsifal in the background, is seeking inspiration as he edits his text, but every now and again he looks out of the window. His attention is caught by the cheerful tones of an ice-cream van, while a noisy group of students in shorts loiters nearby. A general store across the street is already displaying the first swimsuits of the season; the trees on Avenida Callao are in full bloom. Spring, in short, will soon give way to summer: it is November 9, 1989. But this brief moment of distraction is suddenly interrupted by the ringing of the telephone.

"Father Jorge, quick: turn on the TV."

The caller is Guillermo Ortiz, a Jesuit student who lived for a few years in the room next door to the fifty-two-year-old Bergoglio's. Jorge has known him since 1977, when "Guillo" dreamed of becoming a Jesuit and Jorge was the provincial superior. They encountered each other again in the 1980s, one of them a novice, the other the rector of the Colegio Máximo at San Miguel and parish priest of the Church of San José Patriarca. In those days, one of the future priest's duties was to look *after the animals (pigs, sheep, and cattle, among others) that Father Jorge bought and raised to feed the Jesuits at the college, a community of two hundred people.*

But Guillermo was also charged with assembling the children of the neighborhood for Sunday mass. Bergoglio insisted that his priests went down into the streets: future Jesuits had to win over the three barrios that fell within the parish—La Manuelita, Constantini, and Don Alfonso—and be among the people, especially the poorest. In other words, they had to live a faith of the people, committing themselves on the front lines of the parish.

"If you have a minute, take a look at what's on. It's incredible," Guillo continues.

Father Jorge puts down the receiver, turns off the record player, and hurries into the television lounge. It is true: The pictures are coming from Germany, and they are extraordinary. In East Berlin, a river of people has poured into the streets; they are crossing the Berlin Wall, the symbol of the Cold War that has divided the city since 1961. The border crossings have been unexpectedly opened after a press conference during which Günter Schabowski, a Politbüro member and an official of the Central Committee of the Socialist Unity Party of Germany, taken by surprise by a question from a journalist, announced that private citizens could from that moment on leave the German Democratic Republic without the formal authorizations that had until then been required.

Chaos has ensued: young people armed with pickaxes and other tools head for the wall and start to hack at it, to knock it down; whole families get in their cars, while others head for the border on foot. Some decide to bypass the checkpoints and climb over the wall that has caused so much pain and death; others are still terrified that the border guards might open fire on them, as in the past.

The crowd reaches the Brandenburg Gate, a symbol of German pride turned into a propaganda center by communist East Germany. It was not far from here, in front of the Schöneberg town hall, in 1963, that President John F. Kennedy said the famous words, "All free men, wherever they may live, are citizens of Berlin, and therefore, as a free man, I take pride in the words 'Ich bin ein Berliner!'" to cheers and fluttering white handkerchiefs from the crowd.

History was happening before our eyes that afternoon in 1989. The amazing scenes we were watching on our screens were such as I personally had never expected to witness. Young people were dancing, drinking toasts; strangers were hugging one another; whole families were in tears. These were genuinely moving moments, because those people were experiencing the end of oppression and violence. They were rediscovering their freedom.

And soon the Soviet Union would collapse, thanks to *perestroika*, Mikhail Gorbachev's policy of reform. He was a great man, Gorbachev, perhaps one of the finest statesmen the USSR ever had. I admired him because he wanted to reform that world, part of his goal being to prevent further suffering for the people. I remember his daughter and his wife, Raisa, well; she was a remarkable person, as well as a fine philosopher.

I cheered up considerably when I saw the scenes of the Berlin Wall coming down, because Europe was once again finding the longed-for peace that had been absent for so many years. In Argentina we didn't pay too much attention to those events: they concerned another part of the world. Apart from the foreign news services in the first few days, the story of the Berlin Wall didn't feature in television discussions, which focused instead on domestic politics. The presidential election had been won a few months earlier by the Justicialist Party candidate, the hyperliberal Carlos Menem. The son of Syrian immigrants, he was from La Rioja, one of the country's poorest provinces. It was a moment that called for a new way of doing politics, building a culture of democracy and putting forward the idea of solidarity as the root of everything, with the aim of improving citizens' lives. And so there was, of course, much debate about what this new presidency could do for the people.

But every Argentine who, like me, had relatives in Europe certainly paid attention to the news from Germany. At last, the wall that symbolized the ideological partition of the world was coming down! And although we were taken by surprise by those images, and even though we knew that the collapse of the wall had happened suddenly, it is necessary to say that this historic event was made possible by the dedication over the years of many people, by their struggles, by their suffering, sometimes by the sacrifice of their lives. But also, and above all, by prayer. I cannot but think of the role played by John Paul II, whom I had met in Buenos Aires a few years before, in 1987, thanks to the apostolic nuncio, on the occasion of World Youth Day. With his words and his charisma, he had given those people the strength to come together in the struggle for freedom. As early as 1979, in fact, during his first trip back to his Polish homeland, he had raised the consciousness of millions of Eastern Europeans and helped them rediscover hope.

And so this long process led to the fall of that wall in Germany. But there are many walls around the world, probably less famous. Where there's a wall, there is a closed heart; where there's a wall, there is the suffering of a brother and a sister who cannot cross it; where there's a wall, there is division between peoples, and that is not good for the future of humankind. And if we are divided, friendship and solidarity are absent. We must follow the example of Jesus instead, who united everyone with his blood.

But walls are not just physical: when we're not at peace with someone, a wall comes between us. How beautiful the world would be if there were bridges instead of barriers: people could meet and live together under the sign of brotherhood, reducing inequality and expanding freedom and human rights. Wherever there are walls, on the other hand, we see the proliferation of mafias, criminal behavior, dishonest scoundrels exploiting people's weakness and subjecting them to fear and loneliness. We are Christians! So we must love our neighbors unconditionally, without borders, without limits of any kind, going beyond the walls of selfishness and personal or national interests. It is necessary to break the barriers of ideology, which amplify hate and intolerance.

To go back to the fall of the Berlin Wall: One of the many things that struck me as I watched those historic images on Argentine TV was the sincerity and tenderness of the many old people, who had personally experienced great suffering and had been waiting for this moment for many years. When interviewed by journalists after crossing the Iron Curtain, they were so moved they couldn't speak, but they certainly didn't hide their tears.

Like Jesus, they were not afraid of tears. We read in the Gospels that the Lord wept tears for his dead friend Lazarus; he was greatly moved when he saw the throng of people who were like sheep without a shepherd; he wept in his heart when he saw a poor widow taking her only son to be buried. If we don't learn to weep, to give this proof of humanity, we cannot be good Christians.

Father Jorge goes back to his room after watching the broadcast for a few minutes: he wants to finish work on his text before supper. But this is not the only thing for him to do. For example, he also needs to reply to a letter from a former student of his at the College of the Immaculate Conception at Santa Fe. He has placed it in a prominent position on a stack of books because the student has been waiting for a response for a few days already and Jorge does not want to keep him waiting any longer. He has kept in touch with some of the pupils from his courses in literature and psychology, and they still write or call occasionally.

One of them, José has never lost the habit of getting in touch. On this occasion, in a long letter, he recalls an extraordinary classroom encounter with Jorge Luis Borges, the great Argentine writer, invited by Professor Bergoglio to talk to the students about leftist literature. Although more than twenty years have gone by, the ex-student, now a doctor, also asks Father Jorge for some help with a text on the evolutionary theories of the French Jesuit philosopher and paleontologist Pierre Teilhard de Chardin, whose books Father Jorge had recommended at the time. Father Jorge smiles at this unusual request, and sits down at the typewriter to respond to it.

A passage in Father Jorge's reply reads: "When we knew each other in class, the world was still divided into two blocs, my dear José. And on this very day, as I write, that system has collapsed, it has failed, the Berlin Wall is no more."

He puts the record player on again and gets back to work, or at least he tries. His mind returns to the images on the screen: immersed in Wagner's music, he sees again the smiles, the tears of joy, the irrepressible happiness. He remembers too the words of US President Ronald Reagan, which he read in the paper earlier. Visiting West Berlin on June 12, 1987, Reagan had addressed a crowd of nearly fifty thousand in front of the Brandenburg Gate: "Across Europe, this wall will fall, for it cannot withstand faith; it cannot withstand truth. The wall cannot withstand freedom." And it was on this occasion that he gave an unexpected, brusque, and historic piece of advice to the general secretary of the Communist Party of the Soviet Union: "Mr. Gorbachev, open this gate! Mr. Gorbachev, tear down this wall!"

And it really was torn down: the winds of change had finally reached Europe! A few days after the fall of the Berlin Wall, I remember a letter from John Paul II to the bishops of Germany in which, expressing his sense of closeness to the people of Germany and addressing every Catholic in the country, he said he was praying that the Lord, with the intercession of the Virgin Mary, would succeed in realizing "the hopes of humanity for justice, freedom, and internal and external peace." He wrote, "Do everything you can, even if your flock is small, to renew the face of the ground in your country, with the power of God's spirit, together with all men of good will, in unity above all with evangelical Christians."

These words did not fall into a void. The German people took them to heart and walked together in unity, learning again that they were brothers and sisters after their differences had caused death and suffering. I have already mentioned that I was moved by images of old people in tears, but I was touched even more deeply by the sight of members of the same family, previously separated by the Wall, embracing when they finally met in West Berlin. I saw all this with particular joy in my heart, because there had been, in the past, periods of enmity between siblings and cousins in my mother's family, and these had caused me great pain. Maybe this is why my mother and I formed strong bonds with people outside the family, like the ladies who helped my mother with the housework. They were like aunts to me.

I remember Berta, for example, a French lady of sixty. Her daughter had been a dancer and a prostitute, and later married a neighbor of ours. Berta had also been a dancer, in Paris, and though she lived in great poverty and had an uneasy relationship with her daughter, she managed to preserve a unique dignity.

Then there was Concepción María Minuto—we called her Concetta. She came three or four times a week and helped my mother handwash the laundry. I remember her with great affection: she gave me a small medallion of the Madonna that I still wear around my neck. Originally from Sicily, she had spent the war there and had two children, a daughter and a son. She told us that when the time came for the birth of the second child, the boy, she had to walk several miles to catch a train that would take her to the hospital. Her stories revealed terrible poverty, but she was never downhearted and it never dented her simple goodness.

There came a moment, I remember, when her son decided to

start a family of his own and got married. He stayed in Argentina, but Concetta and her daughter moved back to Italy. After a few years, they both returned to Buenos Aires. I was at San Miguel by then, and they came to visit me. The person who received them said to me, "Señora Concepción Minuto is here to see you, Father." But I was busy and, without thinking, told him to say I wasn't available. The next day I was overcome with worry. I kept asking myself, "Why did I behave like that toward a woman I know so well, who has come all the way from Italy and probably had to buy a train ticket to get to San Miguel?" That evening I prayed hard, begging the Lord for forgiveness for my behavior.

A few years later, the daughter came again and left me a note: "I'm Concetta's daughter. I came by to say hello." I called her immediately. In the meantime, the son had started working as a driver in Buenos Aires, and from time to time, when the need arose, I gave him some work. One day I was informed that Concetta was on her deathbed, and I was able to give her spiritual succor in her last hours on this earth. I often think about Concetta: whenever I look at the medallion she gave me I pray for her.

I also fondly remember Señora María de Alsina. She had been a widow for some time and had a daughter with the same name. In fact they were nicknamed *Mari grande* and *Mari chica* (Big Mary and Little Mary). Mari grande worked as a maid for some neighbors, a handsome couple—he was a director in a bank, she a teacher—but they were out at work all day every day. Mari grande was very cultured: she enjoyed reading books on philosophy and listening to opera, so occasionally I liked to invite her to the theater. When she was on her deathbed, her daughter called me out of the blue: "Mom's in hospital, she won't last long." It was nine o'clock at night, and I went to see her immediately and gave her the last rites. Mari chica was left alone after her mother died, and my sister María Elena suggested she come and live with her.

With our maids we had a relationship based on respect: we truly treated them like family. My mother's side of our family, as I previously mentioned, was sadly divided: my mother had five brothers and sisters, and they were constantly feuding. I seldom saw my uncles and aunts. One of my aunts had been put in a care home by her children; one of my uncles I didn't meet until I was an adult, and then only once. Witnessing all these arguments wounded me deeply, I must say.

Unlike the families in Berlin that were separated by the Wall until November 1989, by the grace of God we could see each other any time we wanted, and yet we did not appreciate this divine gift. The family is where we first learn to love, a point I have always clearly understood. But we also know that every family has a cross to bear, because the Lord has provided a way to overcome it: some misunderstandings, some problems can be overcome only by love. Hate, on the other hand, overcomes nothing. This is one of the reasons why I found the images of family members embracing again on the border between East and West Germany so moving: thanks to love, they had overcome that particular division, something my family had not managed to do.

That was one of the last times I watched television. One winter's evening the following year, the day before my transfer to Córdoba, where I was being sent to give spiritual direction to the Jesuit community there, I was watching television in the lounge with my fellow priests. It was July 15, 1990, and some scenes of an adult nature, to put it delicately, were being shown—something that was not good for the heart. Nothing risqué, of course, but when I went back to my room, I said to myself, "A priest cannot look at such things." And so, the following day, during the mass for the feast of the Madonna del Carmelo, I vowed never to watch television again. Only very occasionally do I allow myself to watch: for example, when a new president is sworn in, or I watched briefly once when there had been a plane crash. I switched it on, too, to follow Sunday mass while I was being treated at the Gemelli University Hospital in Rome, but I didn't watch the coronation of Charles III, the new British king, for example, or many other important world events. Not out of disdain, but because I made a vow.

I was in Córdoba for one year, ten months, and thirteen days, until May 1992: a long and dark period of my life. Dark because throughout that period I was carrying a sense of defeat in my heart, because, although obediently accepting the decision of my superiors, I didn't understand why they had sent me there. But a great new page of history was being written in Europe that year.

IX

THE BIRTH OF THE
EUROPEAN UNION

The Jesuit *residencia mayor* is fast asleep. The lights are out in every room, the bell has yet to awaken the priests for lauds and the celebration of the mass. They are still in bed; in fact, it is only four-thirty in the morning. Even outside this enormous stone and concrete structure, with its inner courtyard filled with avocado trees and vines, there is little sign of life. Silence reigns on Calle Caseros, one of the busiest streets in Córdoba, some five hundred miles from Buenos Aires, apart from the rumble of cleaning trucks sweeping the empty streets. The sound of opening shutters echoes in the distance: it is the local baker, Gonzalo, starting his day's work.

At that hour, during the hot Argentine summer of February 1992, only one light is on in the residence, that of the kitchen, and it has been on for some time. Father Jorge, who normally sets his alarm clock for four-thirty, has gotten up earlier than usual. After the time set aside for prayer, he has washed in the communal bathroom at the end of the corridor, then returned to his 120-square-foot room to hurriedly pull on his black robe, polish his shoes, and run downstairs. He has taken a *moment to roll up his sleeves, then to put on a white apron and get to work at the stove. This is not routine; it is a special occasion—a wedding feast.*

Father Jorge has been here for nearly two years, in an exile imposed by the higher echelons of the Society of Jesus in Argentina. After his twelve years occupying important roles within the order, the new leadership has decided to sideline Father Jorge, and his days are spent in silence and prayer, though there is also time for confessions (a few penitents even come from outside the city), writing, and study. And then he helps his older fellow priests, lends a hand in the laundry, and, very occasionally, treats himself to a walk outside the residence to the church of the Barefoot Carmelites or the basilica of Our Lady of Mercy.

That midsummer morning, however, he has decided to give Ricardo and Irma a hand: the former is a handyman at the residence, whom Jorge has known since he was a boy; the latter is the cook and Ricardo's cousin. They have not arrived yet, but Father Jorge has decided to go ahead without them. The wedding feast is for Alejandra, Ricardo's niece. He and Irma were worried, the day before, that they would not be able to manage the menu for this small banquet for friends and family, so the fifty-five-year-old Bergoglio offered to cook the meat and a rice timbale. He has already started boiling the veal in two big pans, and now he is peeling potatoes.

Having once been at the top of his order in Argentina, the Jesuit from Buenos Aires seems to have gone back to the origins of his vocation. He is going through a mysterious period of introspection and searching analysis of his life, alone, far from everyone. A few malicious tongues even suggest he is suffering from a mental disorder. Some Jesuits are waging a campaign to discredit him, spreading the rumor that "Bergoglio is mad," but the truth is very different.

Finally, at half-past five, Ricardo joins him. He lives at the residence, but he had gone out, as he does every morning, to pick up La Nación from the newsstand. He will read it in the common room later. He has brought Father Jorge some ingredients: rice and yogurt for the timbale, which Irma will make with him. Since Ricardo has the newspaper under his arm, Jorge takes a quick look. He pauses briefly on the items about Argentine politics, but among the foreign-news items he notices an editorial about the signing by twelve countries, on February 7, of the Maastricht Treaty, confirming the birth of the European Union. The document, which will enter into force in November 1993, will launch a monetary and economic union and provide for the creation of a central bank, European citizenship, and increased powers for the European Parliament.

Father Bergoglio reads quickly and does not have much time to think about this long article while he is preparing the meal. Having scanned the first few lines, he folds up the paper and goes back to the stove.

I must admit that I didn't spend much time on the news from faraway Europe at first; I didn't really pay much attention to it, perhaps underestimating its importance. Later, with time, I went into it more deeply, reading what the editorial said, and I have to say I liked what I read: the European Union was one of the most beautiful ideas ever conceived by political creativity. Those twelve countries had found the key to successfully achieving subsidiarity, following the path laid out by the founding fathers. As the French Jesuit Father Pierre de Charentenay has pointed out, the union incarnates at the European level what the Church in its documents (such as, for example, John XXIII's social encyclical *Mater et magistra*, Mother and Teacher, or Benedict XVI's *Caritas in veritate*, Charity in Truth) has asked for at the world level: the existence of an authority with multiple areas of competence that can avoid the perils of nationalism.

And this is why Christians are called upon to make their contribution to Europe, today more than ever. They can do this in two ways. First, by remembering that Europe is not made up of numbers but of people. More and more, people talk about figures, quotas, economic indicators, poverty thresholds, instead of talking about citizens, migrants, workers, the poor. Everything is reduced to an abstract idea, so that it can be calmly managed at the political level, without alarmism and without distressing anyone who might be listening. But if nobody talks clearly about people, who have hearts and faces, these discussions will forever remain soulless.

Second, Christians can contribute by rediscovering their sense of belonging to a community. This is the true antidote to individualism, to the widespread tendency these days, especially in the West, to live in solitude. This is a serious matter when it gives rise to a society that is deprived of a sense of belonging, of heritage. We see it, for example, when we face the question of migrants. It seems as if there are two Europes, with some countries believing they can live their lives perfectly well looking after only themselves, leaving other European Union members—like, for example, the Mediterranean countries: Italy, Malta, Spain, Greece, and Cyprus—at the mercy of events, always in crisis. This is not community-building; this is living out a suicidal individualism that can only lead to self-destruction. It is vital that everyone, from north to south, plays their part in welcoming, protecting, advancing, and integrating migrants.

If instead the game is played alone, Europe's citizens will become emotionally detached from its institutions, which can be perceived as distant and careless of individual needs. Europe is primarily a family of peoples. The government at the center must take into account the needs of every country, respecting their identities and intervening if they need help in any area.

When I read the news in *La Nación*, the journalist reminded his readers that Europe, after the fall of the Berlin Wall, needed unity now because it would provide the strength to overcome all conflict and put an end to the divisions of the postwar period. At the time, though, my attention was focused on quite different conflicts: interior ones, the conflicts in my heart.

I had previously lived in Córdoba as a novice in 1958, in the Instituto Sagrada Familia in the Pueyrredón district. In addition to helping some of the old people, my tasks included gathering together the children who lived in the poorest pockets of the neighborhoods around the Hospital Tránsito Cáceres de Allende and teaching them catechism on Saturday afternoon and Sunday morning to prepare them for their first communion. We used to meet in the inner courtyard of the Napoli family's house.

The Napolis were a very generous family, originally Sicilian. They had two children, and every weekend we would all sit under a tree on their patio, ten or so children in all. Sometimes, I would give them some candy afterward, or we would play a game of football. I've never been good at football (when I was a boy they made me play goalie because my teammates said I had legs of wood), but this was a way for them to have some fun and make friends. Each week I would ask them a few questions about the subjects we had discussed the previous time and, if they got the answers right, I would give them sacred picture cards or little medallions of the Madonna. Once or twice I taught them some Italian folk songs, the ones my dad used to listen to at home when we were little, which I therefore knew by heart. I remember "*O sole mio*," for example, or "*Dove sta Zazà?*" and "*Torna piccina*"—hits in the 1940s that were very popular among the Italians in Buenos Aires.

When I returned to Córdoba in 1990, I was *en destierro*, exiled as a punishment, and my situation had changed completely: I had led the Jesuit province of Argentina, I had held posts with big responsibilities, and now I was back as an ordinary confessor, a beautiful and very important office.

Darkness prevailed during that period, a shadow that led me to work on myself and gave me the opportunity to create from my situation the chance of inner purification. Ignatian spirituality was my beacon, but I am certain the Lord granted me this period of crisis in order to test me, and to better read my heart. For nearly two years I thought about my past, my time as provincial, choices made instinctively and subjectively, mistakes born of an attitude that was authoritarian to the point that I was accused of ultraconservatism.

I am increasingly convinced that those years of silence in cell number five of the Córdoba residence served to teach me how to look ahead with serenity. Over the years, some people have placed a little too much emphasis on what happened during that dark period of my life. There were suggestions that I was bullied, that phone calls were not passed on to me, letters not delivered. This is not true; it would be unfair to say such things happened. Some thought it must have been humiliating for me, at my age, to be caring for sick fellow priests, washing them or sleeping by their side to support them, or helping in the laundry; but I did these things instinctively, and I also think this is a fundamental phase in the life of anyone who truly wishes to meet Jesus Christ. Putting oneself at the service of the frail, the poor, the left behind is what every man of God should do, especially if he stands at the pinnacle of the Church: be a shepherd, and smell of sheep.

It is true, though, that I was very closed to others at that time, a little depressed. I spent most of my time in the residence, seldom going out. I had a lot of free time, and between confessions I studied: documents by Pope John Paul II and books by then-Cardinal Joseph Ratzinger for my doctoral thesis; almost all of Ludwig von Pastor's *History of the Popes*—I devoured thirty-six of the forty volumes, not bad going! And, the way things turned out in my life, I must say it served me well.

During those years, too, I started to write two books, *Reflections on Hope* and *Sin and Corruption*. The latter, which was inspired by an article by the journalist Octavio Frigerio titled "Corruption: A Political Problem," includes a passage that, when I read it now, so many years later, brings to mind scandals that have reached as far as the institutions of Europe: "When a corrupt person exercises power, he will always drag others into his corruption and bring them down to his level. Corruption stinks of decay. It is like bad breath: a person who suffers from bad breath is seldom conscious of it. It is others who smell it and must tell him. In the same way, the corrupt person will seldom escape from his condition through pangs of conscience. He has anesthetized the goodness of the soul."

It is now May. After lunch in the refectory, Father Jorge goes up to the first floor and stops, as he does every afternoon, to pray in front of the statuette of St. Joseph holding the infant Jesus in his arms. He places his hand on the glass protecting the saint and bows his head. As they go up and down the stairs his fellow priests see him, absorbed in prayer, still, utterly detached from earthly matters. Once in his room, he gets his typewriter out of the cupboard and sits down at the desk, but a Morse code signal on the bell—dot-dash-dot—tells him he has a phone call. He goes to the telephone cubicle, and the call, an urgent one from Buenos Aires, is put through to him. It is the papal nuncio, Archbishop Ubaldo Calabresi. Father Jorge is not surprised: the two men speak often. From time to time, the nuncio asks for his views on nominations of potential bishops. On this occasion, though, the high-ranking priest does not want to spend much time on the telephone. He wants to meet Father Jorge face-to-face in Córdoba, at the airport, where he has a stopover on his way back to the capital.

"I'll be there, Your Excellency," says Father Jorge, and hangs up.

Father Jorge does not have much time to get to the meeting, but before going to the bus station to catch the airport bus, he finds a moment to stop in the Capilla Doméstica, the domestic chapel, where he says his rosary every day, to say a prayer to the Madonna of Fátima. It is May 13, the day on which the Church remembers the Virgin's first appearance to three Portuguese shepherd boys in 1917. He then goes into the reading room and grabs a newspaper to read on the long bus ride, confident that his brother priests will not mind: there are other papers, and he will return it later in case someone wants to read it after supper.

Once on the bus, sitting beside a woman feeding her baby, Father

Jorge opens the paper and notices a picture of Queen Elizabeth II, who made a historic speech to the European Parliament at Strasbourg the day before, May 12, 1992, following the signing of the Maastricht Treaty in February. The article includes a few extracts from her words, and Father Jorge starts reading with interest:

We are all trying to preserve the rich diversity of European countries because if that diversity is suppressed, we shall weaken Europe not strengthen it. Decisions need to be taken as close to the citizen as is compatible with their success but at the same time we have to strengthen the ability of Europeans to act on a European basis where the nature of a problem requires a European response. That was the necessary balance struck at Maastricht.

Standing here today I am conscious of the differences in national parliamentary traditions across the Community. The British Members will no doubt have brought to the deliberations of this House the vigorous tone of Westminster debate: a style which can be confrontational as some of my ancestors found!

The differences of style and opinion are insignificant against the background of the proven commitment of Europeans today to reconciliation and democracy. Far better the tough talking and controversy of a genuine debate for which this Parliament is a forum than drab uniformity.

Queen Elizabeth was right: one of the tasks of the Europe that was taking shape at the time was to preserve and foster the diversity of its member states. It was an ambitious project, following in the footsteps of the founders of the European Union, with their dream of reconciling differences.

During a visit to Budapest in April 2023, I met representatives of civil society and the diplomatic corps. On that occasion, recalling the speech I had made to the European Parliament at Strasbourg in 2014, I spoke of the need for Europe not to be held hostage by one grouping or another or to fall victim to self-referential authoritarianism, nor to be transformed into a fluid entity that forgets the life of its people. I spoke of the need for harmony, whereby every member feels part of a whole and yet preserves its own identity. Every community brings its own riches, its own culture, its own philosophy, and must be able to maintain those riches, that culture, that philosophy while harmonizing through differences.

The problem is that this no longer happens today. The founders' dream seems very distant. And if I spoke of this in Budapest, it is because I hope my words were heeded both by the Hungarian prime minister, Viktor Orbán, in order that he might understand the great need for unity, and by Brussels—which seems to want to make everything uniform—in order that it might respect the unique features of Hungary.

In a memorable speech to the European Parliament, again in Strasbourg, John Paul II also spoke of this need, but in 1988 and therefore before the fall of the Berlin Wall. He explained the idea clearly, adding that Europeans would need to accept one another despite their different cultural traditions and modes of thought, and furthermore would need to welcome foreigners and refugees and open themselves up to the spiritual riches of people from other continents.

This is a Christian vision, which offers us the chance to find in the story of Europe a coming together of heaven and earth, where heaven signifies openness to the transcendent, to God, who has always marked the people of Europe with favor, and earth represents the concrete and practical ability to face its situation and its problems. The future of Europe—the old Europe, tired and sterile—depends on the rediscovery of the crucial link between these two elements. A Europe that is no longer capable of opening itself to the transcendent dimension of life is a Europe that risks gradually losing its soul, and even the humanistic spirit it loves and defends.

The European Union must awake from its torpor. It must once again put forward a new humanism based on three competencies: to integrate, to engage in dialogue, to flourish. After all, the old continent is quite capable of starting from scratch if necessary. It showed this after World War II, when everything needed to be rebuilt. And it succeeded because hope never left the hearts of those who were building this new political idea of placing human beings at the center of everything. In this context it is vital that thought is given to training people to read the signs of the times and interpret the European project within the story of today. Otherwise, nothing but the technocratic paradigm will remain, which doesn't interest the younger generation and will signal the end of the project.

To go back to the afternoon of May 13, 1992: My bus had finally reached the airport, slightly early in fact. I believe what happened during my meeting with the nuncio, a great man to whom I owe so much, is now in the public domain. At first he talked about other matters, asking me a series of questions on a wide range of subjects. And then, unexpectedly, as he arrived at the gate for his flight, he gave me the news that would change my life: "I'm pleased to tell you that you have been named auxiliary bishop of Buenos Aires by John Paul II. Your nomination will be made public in seven days, on May 20. Please don't breathe a word to anyone."

I was stunned. I stopped in my tracks, tongue-tied, unable to say anything, as always when someone says something unexpected to me. It still happens today! Anyway, I respected the apostolic messenger's instructions, beginning at supper in the refectory with my superiors and brother priests that very evening: the news remained secret until it was published. Cardinal Antonio Quarracino, archbishop of Buenos Aires, whom I had been privileged to meet a few years earlier, when I was leading spiritual exercises and he was archbishop of La Plata, had asked for me to be his close collaborator. And so I became one of four auxiliaries chosen by him.

After my ordination as a bishop in the city's cathedral, opposite Plaza de Mayo, the archbishop sent me to Flores as an episcopal vicar. This was the district of my childhood, where I had grown up. Now, at age fifty-five, I was returning as a pastor. There was a feeling of great celebration. My period of darkness was just a memory; the Lord wanted me to start on a new path, near the people, taking the word and the comfort of Christ to the neediest families in the *villas miserias*, or shantytowns.

During those years I came to know a priest with a vocation to work in the slums, Father José María Di Paola, or Father Pepe. In 1994, by which time I had been named vicar general, I sent him to be a parish priest in Ciudad Oculta, Hidden City, and then, a few years later, Villa 21, both blighted districts of Buenos Aires. He worked with children and the indigent, and I used to go and see him often because, as I have said before, I have always considered it vital for pastors to be among their flock. If necessary, for example, if another priest was sick, I helped out with mass or confession. I always tried to attend the processions organized by the *curas villeros*, the shantytown priests brought together by Father Pepe, walking among those seekers of Jesus: the people's piety is the Church's immune system.

These were among the best times of my life. Walking those dusty alleyways, I myself found the Lord, and He told me not to abandon those poor souls. But I also spent time listening to their stories, accepting invitations into their dwellings for a cup of *mate* and a chat, like old friends. Don't think these were amusing stories, and that we had a good laugh: I wiped away many tears, because those people lived in the midst of poverty, in homes built of loose bricks and corrugated iron, surrounded by feral dogs, with no drinking water. Criminals and drug traffickers are the true rulers of these disadvantaged areas; children, left to their own devices, are dragged into the drug trade from an early age. The presence of the Church was therefore crucial, and it remains necessary today, to carry out its work of prevention and guidance, particularly of the very young, toward a clean future far from such soul-corrupting evils. The Church's work on the margins is so important, especially where the state is absent! Priests and nuns, with their presence and their words, can make all the difference, helping the young in particular to start out on the right path, so as to avoid getting trapped in traumatic spirals that could destroy their lives forever. Listening to such people patiently and with an open mind—parents in crisis, children of the streets— really can change things for the better. I have experienced it myself, by listening and talking to hundreds of people at the margins to this day.

A few years later, in 1997, the papal nuncio surprised me for a second time: At the end of a meal like many others, he ordered some cake and a bottle of champagne for a toast. I asked if it was his birthday. "No," he said, "it's not my birthday, this is for you!" Again I was speechless. I didn't understand. And then he continued, "Starting on June 3, you are the new archbishop coadjutor of Buenos Aires."

In essence, I had acquired the right to succeed Cardinal Quarracino, the archbishop of Buenos Aires, when he reached retirement age and stepped down. Unfortunately, Cardinal Quarracino he died a few months later, before he turned seventy-five, the canonical age of retirement, and on February 28, 1998, I suddenly found myself at the helm of the huge archdiocese.

I carried out this very delicate role with a single huge priority: to be at the service of the Argentine people, especially those overwhelmed by poverty and wretchedness. It was a challenge, and a great gift, to be able to carry the gospel of Jesus Christ both to the powerful, whose ears are often stopped because they are distracted by other interests and a society that is increasingly "in flux," and to the left behind, the Lord's preferred people, who have taught me so much with their love-seeking eyes and deafening silences. During those wonderful years I touched hands that were rough and scarred, the hands of starving people who had not tasted food for days. Hands that had stolen to feed children, hands that sought help to change for the better. I caressed the faces of people young and old, abandoned at the roadside without hope, the faces of women robbed of their dignity, the faces of terrified fathers, and the faces of mothers crushed by indifference. The faces of children whose future had been stolen from them. And in all of them I always found the one Savior, Jesus Christ, who is the way, the truth, and the life.

It is a gift. Everyone should know it, everyone should feel it: let us get our hands dirty, let us give some sense to our existence by seeking God among the poor, touching their hands, looking into their eyes. By standing among the invisible people of our cities, welcoming and supporting them, we will find our reward, and our lives will be better. Even now, when as pope I am far from the streets of Argentina, I know this is the only way, alongside prayer, to feel the presence of the Lord every day: all that is needed is a meal with the poor; all that is needed is an encounter, a glance, to rediscover the strength to move forward.

Knowing that Buenos Aires was historically a seat of cardinals, I expected the purple to follow my elevation, and it did. In 2001, John Paul II selected me as a cardinal along with another forty-three brothers. This was yet another new thing, and I experienced it religiously, praying with the evangelical certainty that every rise brings with it a fall. The consistory took place in St. Peter's Square, in Rome, on February 21. Nobody dreamed that in that same year the world would be convulsed by the September 11 terrorist attacks on the United States.

X

THE TERRORIST ATTACKS
ON SEPTEMBER 11

There is a constant coming and going in the archbishop's office: staff, cleaners, technicians, attendants, priests, nuns. Some have been at work since seven-thirty in the morning, while others are just starting a day's work that will end late that night. It is a day like any other in Avenida Rivadavia in Buenos Aires: boxes of stationery are being unloaded from a truck parked in front of the building, an electrician on a stepladder is replacing spent lightbulbs in some of the curia's offices.

Among those offices is that of Señora Otilia, the archbishop's secretary. Between cigarettes, she is listening to the electrician with one ear and listening with the other for any calls that might come in for the cardinal, Archbishop Bergoglio. She is a little anxious because, like every day, there is an endless list of people coming to be received by the man recently raised to the purple, and she will have to ensure they are welcomed. She does not know these people, she does not have their phone numbers; the appointments have almost all been made directly with the archbishop, who has a personal diary that he fills in himself.

On that freezing September morning, Father Jorge—as many

continue to call him, rather than Your Eminence—arrived early, as in fact he does every day, carrying his black bag and dressed in the clothes of a humble cleric. He lives in a small apartment carved out of the third floor of the building: a bedroom with a private bathroom, a room with a desk and a bookshelf, and behind it a tiny chapel. In contrast to many other cardinals, he has not filled his wardrobe with made-to-measure cardinal's vestments: he uses the ones previously worn by Cardinal Quarracino, mended and altered by nuns.

On a shelf in the bedroom he has a statuette of St. Francis of Assisi; a picture of "the Little Flower," St. Thérèse of Lisieux, to whom he is devoted; and a large crucifix, in front of which he prays every morning, leaning a hand against the wall. He has retained a sleeping St. Joseph from his days as the Jesuit provincial: it is on another piece of furniture, and sometimes he slips under it pieces of paper on which he has noted tricky situations he needs to deal with.

The enormous, patrician archbishop's residence, some twelve miles outside the city center in the elegant Olivos district, is available to him, but he has turned it into a center for spiritual exercises. The new cardinal has also forgone the historic office of the archbishop, establishing himself instead in a smaller and plainer room and turning the much grander room that is his due into a store for books, objects, and food-stuffs to be given as gifts: he has kept the habit of giving away gifts he receives to those in greater need. He uses the metro or buses to move about the city and therefore does not need the limousine and driver either. He has found the latter a new job.

On one of his trips on public transport the day before, the sixty-four-year-old encountered a small group of young teachers. After a short conversation, they asked, somewhat cheekily, for an audience the following day, on the occasion of the Day of the Teacher. In Argentina, schoolteachers are celebrated every September 11, in memory of Domingo Faustino Sarmiento, a writer and former president of Argentina, who dedicated much of his life to the development of public education in his country. When he got back home, Bergoglio checked his diary and, that very evening, called one of the young people to confirm the appointment for the next day. And now they are all on the list of morning audiences that his secretary is holding in her hand.

It is twenty past ten. A small delegation of businesspeople has just left the cardinal's office and the door is open again. From his room, Father Jorge hears a murmur of animated conversation, even a few raised voices: there is an unusual amount of movement, with people coming out of their offices. He goes to his own door and sees a small group of curia colleagues standing motionless in front of a small television. As he approaches, he sees a scene that might be from a movie. But it is reality: a special edition of the news is showing images of one of the Twin Towers of the World Trade Center in Manhattan, the North Tower, in flames. The American correspondent is reporting, by telephone, that an airplane has crashed into the skyscraper.

Father Jorge checks his wristwatch: it is half past ten, time for his next visitor, but what he is seeing on the television is so unbelievable he feels paralyzed. No sooner does he ask "What happened?" than another airplane crashes into the South Tower. It all happened about an hour before: Argentine TV has put together this special edition at top speed, and now it is receiving recordings from the main US networks.

"Mother of God," are his first and only words, uttered under his breath. He closes his eyes, bowing his head and quickly pulling himself together in prayer. A cloud of dark smoke fills the streets of Manhattan.

Caked in dust, people struggle to get away; some throw themselves out of the burning towers, while others, who have managed to escape from the buildings, ask for help, their faces covered with blood. The wailing of sirens from fire trucks and ambulances can be heard, along with the sound of weeping and screaming. An apocalyptic scene: the United States is under attack. The death toll will rise to nearly three thousand.

My heart is in pieces at the sight of these images. We were witnessing something horrifying, something we would never even have imagined. My first thoughts were for all those poor people in the towers, then their families, who would be experiencing days of intense drama. I collected myself in prayer, asking the Lord to relieve those people's suffering and welcome the victims of these inhuman actions into His presence. I wept for them. That morning I saw the video of the second plane flying into the tower; later, I was shown the pictures of the first plane and the attack on the Pentagon, as well as the plane that crashed in Pennsylvania. The faces of those stunned, bewildered Americans, covered in dust or being rescued or escaping from the debris, have stayed with me. What suffering.

Every time I think of those people, I am reminded of the images of wars all over the world, and the suffering of those who find themselves beneath the bombs. On that day, September 11, 2001, war arrived in the heart of the West. It was no longer something that concerned only the Middle East or a few countries in Africa or Asia, often little known to the inhabitants of the so-called First World: the United States, known to be one of the world's great powers, had been attacked.

At first, when the first plane struck the skyscraper, everyone thought it was an accident, but then, with the second, the truth became obvious: a terrorist attack was in progress, and the world was being plunged again into the nightmare of war. At the time, a few conspiracy theorists even claimed—and wrote it in newspapers or on the web—that on that morning all the Jews who worked in the World Trade Center had stayed away because they had been warned of what was going to happen. This serious allegation caused an even deeper wound than the events of that day, because it pointed the finger at an innocent people that has historically been the victim of a genocide that still cries out for vengeance in the sight of God. The despair was shared by everyone, regardless of their religion. Tears of agony were shed on that day, in the face of fratricide, in the face of our inability to resolve our differences through dialogue; it was an unjust and senseless waste of innocent lives through an unprecedented act of violence, the negation of any authentic religiosity.

It is blasphemous to use the name of God to justify slaughter, murder, terrorist attack, the persecution of individuals and entire populations—as some still do. Nobody can invoke the name of the Lord to wreak evil. The clergy's task must be to denounce and expose all attempts to justify any kind of hate in the name of religion, and to condemn anyone who propagates this idolatrous distortion of God.

On September 11, death seemed to have won the day, but a tiny flame of hope still flickered in the darkness: the flame of love. In the midst of that searing pain, humanity showed its best face, that of goodness and heroism. Let us remember those who came forward to support the first responders, those who gave out food and water, those who kept businesses open to provide help to the police and firefighters, those who brought blankets and basic necessities, some from far away. Let us remember the helping hands held out in a city that could sometimes seem focused entirely on profit, but which instead showed itself capable of generating solidarity with everyone.

At that moment, differences of religion, blood, origin, politics were torn down in the name of a sense of brotherhood that has no borders. They were all Americans, and proud of it. And I think of the New York City police officers and firefighters who entered the towers, when they were on the point of collapse, to save as many lives as humanly possible. They risked everything; they put other people's lives ahead of their own. Some of them died in the line of duty; others managed to save many people while surrounded by devastation.

In 2015, I paid a visit to the 9/11 Memorial at Ground Zero for an interfaith meeting: together, we prayed to the Lord to strengthen us in our hope and to grant us the courage to work for a world in which peace and love can reign between nations and in the hearts of all people. I was able to meet the families of some of the first responders who had died in the line of duty. In their eyes I saw overwhelming pain, but also the strength of memory and love. Many of them had forgiven, in honor of loved ones who certainly wouldn't have sought revenge. Our commitment to peace must be habitual, particularly in those countries where war seems never to end.

On the day after the attacks, September 12, 2001, we all prayed in communion with Pope John Paul II, who during his general audience beseeched God to come to our aid as we faced "the horror of destructive violence" in those days of mourning and innocent suffering. In his speech, the pope said we were living through a dark day in the history of humanity, and that what had happened in the United States was a terrible affront to the dignity of all human beings. Some fellow cardinals and I had the opportunity to discuss this with him ourselves at the end of the month, when I went to the Vatican for the General Assembly of the Synod of Bishops, which, as the name suggests, is dedicated to the figure of the bishop.

As winter gives way to spring in Buenos Aires, autumn in Rome offers a spectacular gift: the yellowing leaves on the trees lining the Tiber dance in the air, caressed by the wind. The sun's golden reflections mingle with the warm colors of the season, while the shadows lengthen on the banks of the river. The majestic statues on the Ponte Sant'Angelo are mirrored in the water. The few figures that can be seen, wrapped in dark coats and walking briskly, seek shelter from the now-chilly gusts of wind.

Father Jorge arrived in Rome about ten days ago. This is his third visit to Italy since the February consistory. He stopped briefly in Turin to visit relatives, staying at the home of his cousin, Carla, and has now come to the capital to attend the synod, which will last until the end of October. The poetry of the picture-postcard views is shattered by car horns and the chaos of the morning: the Lungotevere is at a standstill, with motorbikes weaving through the endless line of cars. A taxi driver rages at another driver through his window, while a bus driver, one of many forced to crawl through the jam, tries to keep a lid on a group of students who are complaining about the delay. Tourists, meanwhile, swarm toward St. Peter's Square on foot; many take pictures of the Tiber, trying to get the best possible shot to show their friends when they get home.

The magazines and newspapers in the newsstands are given over to the September 11 terrorist attacks: they are still being discussed, even in Italy. And on October 7, barely a month after that tragedy, Operation Enduring Freedom was launched in Afghanistan by the US government and its allies: air strikes in support of the rebels and ground strikes following the refusal of the Taliban leader, Mullah Omar, to hand over Osama bin Laden, the head of Al-Qaida and the brains behind the attacks on the United States. Once again, in short, the world is at war.

Cardinal Bergoglio glances at the papers as he hurries past. Fortunately he is not held up in traffic because he is on foot, as he is every morning: it is a roughly twenty-five-minute walk, beneath Rome's pale autumn sun, from the priests' residence off Piazza Navona to the Vatican, where the Synod of Bishops is in progress. The Argentine cardinal is general rapporteur for the meeting, and he is spending every day working closely with bishops and cardinals from all over the world to draft the Propositiones that will summarize the participants' interventions and the outcome of their discussions.

Bergoglio intervened in the assembly himself, on October 2, to share his thoughts on the figure of the bishop, expressing his opinion that pastors should be predisposed toward the poor and toward a missionary spirit, and should above all be prophets of justice, particularly for those who have been discarded by society. The porteño, or Buenos Aires native, gave his short speech to the meeting in his mother tongue, taking up the thread of a 1996 meditation of his, written on the occasion of the spiritual exercises he had led for Spanish bishops: specifically, it describes the difference between pastors who watch their people and those who keep watch over them:

Supervising is more about guidance in doctrine and habits, in their expression and practice; whereas keeping watch means ensuring that salt and light may be found in their hearts. Watching suggests being alert to imminent danger, whereas keeping watch means patiently enduring the ways in which the Lord continues to prepare for the salvation of His people. To watch, it is sufficient to be alert, astute, quick; to keep watch requires the humility, the patience, and the constancy of tested love. . . . Supervising and watching, suggest a certain level of necessary control; keeping watch speaks to us of hope, the hope of the merciful Father who keeps watch over the progress of his children's hearts.

During breaks in their work over the next few days, brother priests approach Bergoglio. Some compliment him on his intervention; others want to challenge him on this or other subjects. But there is also time to comment on the news in the papers, including the United States–led "war on terror" after the attack on the Twin Towers.

In a sense, my nomination as assistant relator general was linked to the terrorist attacks, in that the synod's relator general was Cardinal Edward Egan, archbishop of New York, who a few days earlier, on October 11, had asked the pope's permission to go home for ceremonies to mark the first month after the attacks. Apart from the commemoration itself, Egan felt strongly that it was his duty to stand with the wounded populace at that moment, principally to console the families of victims and rescuers who had died in service. Despite his important assignment at the Vatican, he didn't hesitate to ask to return to the United States, and John Paul II, who attended all our meetings, of course agreed without difficulty. The pope then named me in Egan's place. I must confess that I was a little apprehensive about the task at first, but it all went well, thanks be to God.

Every day, I worked side by side with the special secretary of the synod, Monsignor Marcello Semeraro, then bishop of Oria and now a cardinal. We conducted the General Assembly, without a hitch, right to the end. During breaks, we talked with fellow bishops about the war in Afghanistan, the US offensives, and the need for Islamic leaders to join in condemnation of the serious attacks that had been carried out in the name of God. The silence of certain fundamentalists had, in fact, created a sense of unease where our Muslim brothers were concerned, and unfortunately this persisted for several years. Although I did not share her views, I read and was struck by the comments of the Italian journalist Oriana Fallaci on this subject.

But as Christians and Muslims, we are called to walk side by side, to engage in dialogue, aware of our cultural and religious differences and not seeing each other as enemies. We must welcome our brothers and sisters of the Islamic faith as traveling companions; we must cooperate for a more just and equal world, recognizing fundamental rights and freedoms, especially of religion, transforming ourselves into builders of civilizations. There exist those who breathe hate and incite violence, but we must respond with love and education, guiding younger generations toward the good, so that they may transform the air that has been poisoned by hatred into the oxygen of brotherhood.

In the United Arab Emirates in 2019, with my brother Ahmad

al-Tayeb, the Grand Imam of Al-Azhar, I signed the *Document on Human Fraternity for World Peace and Living Together*. Among other things, we said: "We, . . . on the basis of our religious and moral responsibility, . . . call upon ourselves, upon the leaders of the world as well as the architects of international policy and world economy, to work strenuously to spread the culture of tolerance and of living together in peace; to intervene at the earliest opportunity to stop the shedding of innocent blood and bring an end to wars, conflicts, environmental decay, and the moral and cultural decline that the world is presently experiencing." We intended this to be a heartfelt appeal to rediscover the values of peace, justice, goodness, and human brotherhood, confirmation of the importance of these values as a sheet anchor for all people, and to spread them everywhere.

There is a great need for a sense of shared humanity in order to overcome our suspicions of those who are different from ourselves and to stop the persecution by fanatics of so many Christians in the world who are forced to flee their homes. These are men and women who, like the earliest Christan communities, escape and preserve their faith like a treasure that gives meaning to their lives. Since September 11 we have become familiar with a new world in which fear has sometimes prevailed and the horror of persecution continues at the hands of terrorists: we have seen them slaughter innocent Christians to the sound of complicit silence, particularly from the countries that could have stopped them but didn't.

But the history of the Church has always been marked by events like these: the persecution began against Jesus and continues today with new martyrs bearing witness to the gospel. To those brothers and sisters, the martyrs of our times, who are much more numerous than they were in the early days, I wish to say strongly: do not be afraid to bear witness to the Lord with love through your actions; do not allow yourselves to be frightened by those who seek to nullify the force of evangelism with arrogance and violence. They can kill the body, but they have no power over the soul.

To go back to the Synod of Bishops that opened barely a month after the terrorist attacks in the United States: It was clear to all of us, bishops and cardinals, that a geopolitical revolution would take place quite soon. The equilibrium of the world would change in the face of threats and attacks in the name of a holy war. The narrative was in the hands of a few terrorist groups composed of religious fanatics, and in that context more than ever, the Church was called upon to act to promote peace and dialogue between religions.

Our discussions on the subject remained inconclusive. I returned to Argentina at the end of October and went back to my day-to-day life. I must confess that I tried to stay as close as possible to my flock, leaving Buenos Aires only if I had crucial and unavoidable obligations elsewhere. After all, my mission was to stand with my people and watch over them.

A few months later, in December 2001, Argentina would be thrown into turmoil by a serious economic crisis that brought the country to the brink of collapse, with social disorder and great political uncertainty. It was just the first alarm bell for what would happen to the world in the years to come: the global recession that changed the lives of millions.

XI

THE GREAT
ECONOMIC CRISIS

Buenos Aires Metropolitan Cathedral is steeped in silence. The only sound is that of some footsteps on the Venetian-mosaic floor. They belong to María Paz, who has arrived after a chilly half-hour walk from Plaza Constitución, where she has lived with her husband, Marcelo, for some years. On rainy nights in that September of 2008, the couple seek protection in the bus station's shelters, but it is not only rain that they fear: as night falls, the square is taken hostage by unscrupulous drug dealers and pimps, and their lives are in constant danger.

Marcelo is a cartonero*: by day, he rummages through the city's garbage cans in search of paper and cardboard to sell and scrape together a little money, along with many other* cartoneros *born of the economic crisis that has convulsed Argentina since December 2001. María Paz, for her part, spends her days looking for casual work here and there, almost always without success. Wrapped in a threadbare blanket that does not really protect her from the biting winter cold, she was awakened at dawn, as she is every morning, by the noise of the first buses departing. She washed her face in a drinking fountain and decided to* go to the cathedral; there are rumors among many of the homeless that early in the morning it is possible to meet Cardinal Bergoglio there, offering confession to the faithful like an ordinary priest.

She has met him in person only once, the previous July 1, when she and Marcelo went to the parish of Our Lady Mother of Emigrants, in the district of La Boca, where the cardinal celebrated a mass organized by the Movement of Excluded Workers, a people's organization that unites cartoneros, sex workers, undocumented migrants, victims of human trafficking, the homeless, and others who live on the fringes of society.

The woman's face is marked by the passage of time; her hair is gray, her hands red and stiff with cold. Inside the cathedral she finds comfort in the flame of a candle burning in front of the statue of Our Lady of Bonaria. She sits down in a pew, as highly polished as the eighteenth-century wooden confessionals. One of these is occupied by a priest wearing a stole over his shoulders, and he is ready to take confession from anyone who needs it.

María Paz has no major sins to confess. She just wants a priest to listen to her and offer a few words of comfort.

"It's all right, I don't bite." The voice comes from the confessional, and it is that of Cardinal Bergoglio. Faced with the woman's hesitancy—she is nervous and intimidated—the cardinal emerges from the small central door and sits on a nearby pew, gesturing to her to come closer.

The two start talking, and stay there for more than half an hour. Mainly it is María Paz telling the story of her life, about her husband Marcelo, and how the 2001 crisis destroyed their world.

"Just this morning," the archbishop tells her quietly, "I was hearing that it's happening in the United States too. The economic crisis touches everyone sooner or later. But it's good that you stay together despite your problems. That shows you are true Christians. You give each other strength. Come with me," the cardinal continues, pressing into her hands some money he has taken from his trouser pocket. "I'll give you something hot to eat. You need it."

María Paz is confused. She does not know whether to cry, laugh, or hug him. Instinctively, she kneels and kisses his hand. The Jesuit gets her to her stand up and, having offered her some tea and cookies, takes his leave to head back to the curia.

"Do we need to worry about this, Your Eminence?" asks Gustavo, a member of his staff, whom he meets at the entrance to the archbishop's building. "I've seen on the internet that a bank has failed in America, and a crisis is building."

It is September 15. A little before dawn that morning, one of the biggest US investment banks, Lehman Brothers, declared bankruptcy. It was sunk by subprime mortgages, speculative loans granted to customers who did not have the resources or guarantees to repay them. The huge industry the bank created turns out to have a boomerang effect: Lehman, which has profited ruthlessly from these loans, itself falls victim to financial speculation. The company's shares collapse; the Federal Reserve Bank and the US secretary of the treasury find a buyer among the biggest names on Wall Street, but at the last moment it pulls out of the deal. There is no choice but to default: twenty-five thousand employees of the banking colossus are laid off; the US stock market collapses, infecting markets in South America, Europe, and Asia. Long lines of panicked people try to withdraw their savings at *cash machines. The US property bubble has burst, triggering a crisis that will lead to a global recession.*

There had, in fact, been a chain reaction all over the world, and over the years it generated fresh inequalities and new poverty, particularly in the most industrialized countries. I can still see the despairing faces of that American bank's employees, men and women carrying their personal effects out of the building in cardboard boxes. I prayed to the Lord that He might console them; I prayed for all the people who had lost everything from one moment to the next: their life's savings, their dream of a home of their own, everything up in smoke in a few seconds.

Visitors to New York at that time told me about long lines in front of food banks: unemployment had reached levels never seen before, and the people lining up for a piece of bread or a hot meal included former managers and chief executives of companies that had been speculating with other people's livelihoods until a few days before. The engine of social mobility, which in the past had helped many to escape a life of desperation, had completely broken down all over the world. Even today it is just a mirage for many people. The current economic system is unsustainable: I have said many times that this economy kills. We can't waste any more time!

We are living at a time when there is an urgent need to rethink the economic model and rethink ourselves, by trying to see things through the eyes of the poor and discarded, working out how to combat increasing inequality and how to overcome our indifference to such people, who are our brothers and sisters. To have hope in the future, along with the young, we must develop a different economic model, based on fairness and a sense of shared humanity; an economic model that gives people life instead of killing them, that doesn't aim to speculate with their lives but puts them front and center; an economy that is inclusive and humanizing, that takes care of creation instead of plundering it.

In my encyclical *Fratelli tutti* (Brothers and Sisters All), I stated in this context: "The right of some to free enterprise or market freedom cannot supersede the rights of peoples and the dignity of the poor. . . . The marketplace, by itself, cannot resolve every problem, however much we are asked to believe this dogma of neoliberal faith." I would like to make it clear that these words are not intended to condemn the market, but to demonstrate the risks and consequences that the system has generated and continues to generate. Let us consider, for example, the introduction of markets into fields where resources had previously been managed in a communal way.

From an ethical standpoint that is a friend to both humanity and the environment, the challenge will be to "civilize" the market, asking it to place itself at the service of human development as a whole, and not just to be efficient at producing wealth. We must be united, all of us, in combating systemic growth in inequality and exploitation of the planet—just some of the factors increasing the gap between the center and the periphery, the products of a system with profit as its sole objective. On the contrary, as I said to members of The Economy of Francesco, the international movement that brings together young economists, entrepreneurs, and activists engaged in an inclusive dialogue for a new economy, it is necessary to accept, structurally, that "the poor have sufficient dignity to sit at our meetings, participate in our discussions, and bring bread to their own tables. It is about much more than 'social assistance' or 'welfare': we are speaking of a conversion and transformation of our priorities and of the place of others in our policies and in the social order."

The explosion of the economic crisis in the United States struck me in particular because I had seen from up close the effects that a situation like that can have. In December 2001, Argentina was plunged into this same nightmare: banks were collapsing, current accounts had been frozen by the government, and many businesses had failed. A near-majority of Argentines had fallen into poverty.

Just before Christmas 2001, we opened an Argentine round table of national dialogue at the headquarters of Caritas Internationalis, to bring together the country's civic and religious leaders in an effort to find a solution for the good of the people. I was present as chair of the Argentine Episcopal Conference and archbishop of Buenos Aires, but President Fernando de la Rúa also attended, and demonstrators who had gathered in Plaza de Mayo objected to his presence. Later, when he declared a state of siege, millions of people descended into the streets, banging on saucepans and demanding that he step down. The president's official residence, the Casa Rosada, was targeted, and de la Rúa fled in a helicopter. He resigned a few hours later.

As a church, meanwhile, we moved to offer our services in the months that followed. We had to be a kind of field hospital for the needy: parish offices remained open day and night to provide accommodations for people who had been left homeless; we asked those of the faithful who had the means to bring essential items to mass, or directly to Caritas, for the poor; we opened medical centers to give out free medication and installed gas-fired ovens under bridges to bake bread and distribute it. Temporary buildings to house the homeless were put up, and new social projects were launched to offer a future to people who had lost everything. Volunteers had to have one sole objective: to put the human person first and, above all, to listen to his or her needs.

I want to emphasize the importance of listening, because so many crises, like the one that started in September 2008, could definitely have been averted on several occasions if the big people, instead of thinking of their own profits and the god of money, had listened, even just once, to the voice of the little people. I also spoke of the importance of listening—in connection with these events—a few weeks later, in October, on the occasion of a pilgrimage that is very well known in Argentina.

The side of Plaza Belgrano facing the sanctuary of the Basilica of Our Lady of Luján is crowded with a mass of young people: there are at least a million of them, and they have walked for more than fifteen hours to make the thirty-fourth annual pilgrimage to the nation's patron saint. The procession left the sanctuary of San Cayetano, in the Buenos Aires district of Liniers, at noon on October 4, carrying the imagen cabecera of the Madonna, a miniature copy of the original statue. Along the way, between hymns and prayers, volunteers gave aid and support to those in need; many stopped for a short rest at roadside stalls selling fruit, chilled water, snacks, souvenirs, and religious items— particularly rosary beads.

Some have joined in order to ask the Virgin for a miracle, some out of simple faith; others hope for the grace of finding a job or buying a home, after losing everything because of the economic crisis. Still others are looking for love, and trust in the Madonna, or hope to graduate at the end of the academic year, which might be a miracle too big even for Our Lady of Luján.

After an arduous walk of more than thirty-five miles, the pilgrims have at last reached their destination: it is six-forty-five the following morning, Sunday, October 5, 2008. The original statue of the Madonna, clad in a long blue cloak, awaits the faithful in front of the sanctuary for one of the most moving moments of the pilgrimage: the meeting of the two statues and the act of devotion by everyone present.

Cardinal Bergoglio is there also, celebrating mass in the square as he does every year, along with other bishops and priests. He too is a devotee of the Virgin of Luján. The theme of this year's pilgrimage is "Mother, teach us to listen," and in his homily the cardinal invites the faithful to reflect, giving them words of hope:

How many problems in life could be resolved if we would learn to listen, if we would learn to listen to each other. Because to listen to another means to spend a little time in their life, in their heart, and not to walk on by as if they don't concern us. And life accustoms us to walking on by, to being uninterested in the life of the other, in what the other has to say to us, or answering before they have finished speaking. If in the environments we inhabit we would learn to listen . . . how things would change. How things would change in the family if husband, wife, parents, children, siblings would learn to listen to each other . . . but we tend to reply before knowing what a person wants to say to us. Are we afraid to listen? How many things would change at work if we learned, as a people, to listen. . . . Mother, we ask you to teach us to remain silent in order to welcome those who need to tell us about their lives, often filled with suffering.

The applause in the square goes on for a long time. The crowd includes many cartoneros, many inhabitants of shantytowns, brought here by their priests; there are people who have nothing left but tears after watching their businesses fail. The global economic crisis has changed the lives of many Argentines, but fortunately it has not profoundly affected the much-tested financial underpinnings of the country. It is true that the stock market suffered a major backlash, unleashing moments of hysteria in the world of high finance. The prices of exports such as soybean oil, grain, pellet fuel, and fuel oil fell, and the peso was devalued by 10 percent against the dollar, but the effects were not as disastrous as in some parts of the world, mainly because of the absence of foreign capital in the country.

In fact, we had already suffered the worst blow in 2001. When the crisis hit the US banks, only certain sectors in Argentina were thrown into turmoil; others, fortunately, having already been stripped to the bone during the previous crisis, were unaffected. I recall the words of Pope Benedict XVI, remarking on the Lehman Brothers default and the resulting global recession, he said that the collapse of great US credit institutions demonstrated the fundamental mistake: the true God had once again been eclipsed by greed and idolatry and turned into the false god Mammon, earthly riches idolized and exalted.

Indeed, what was happening in the United States, which would go on to affect the world's biggest economies, was caused by the sick mentality of people who tried, and are still trying today, to bleed the weakest among us dry, to make money out of money. They still haven't grasped that, for the good of humanity, central to everything must be work, the only true engine that is capable of driving the economy and conferring dignity on human beings. If an idol is placed at the center, money, the system will not be able to create new jobs and will instead cause an increase in unemployment and rob millions of people of their futures.

Where there is no work, I'm sorry to say, there is no dignity, considering that it is harder and harder these days for a young person to find a steady job with a decent wage that covers ever-rising rents and sky-high mortgages that often need to be backed by parents. When these costs are borne by young people themselves, the situation can become even more serious. It is dramatic, and one of the consequences of this sick economy, and I would like to repeat that politics should act on precisely these matters, because without corrective interventions the free market goes wild and produces greater and greater inequality. We must ask, too: If the young can't find work and remain unemployed, who will pay the pensions of people who have worked their whole lives?

I remember that many young men and women on the pilgrimages to Luján asked the Madonna to grant them the grace to find a job, no matter how small, as long as it was respectable. On the other hand, it is offensive to see people complain when faced with a good and honest job offer. How can they not understand that there's a line outside—a line of people who are willing to accept half the salary on offer?

How many prayers have I heard in front of the miraculous Virgin, how many requests for the grace to escape the crisis or a period of unemployment? During those gatherings we breathed an air of goodness; the Holy Spirit was there in our midst. I remember that river of people emerging from the sanctuary to receive confession. I always made myself available, like all the other priests, to take confessions from six o'clock on Saturday afternoon until ten-fifteen at night. Then I would go away to have a sandwich or a slice of pizza and try to get some sleep, setting my alarm for one o'clock on Sunday morning, at which time I would go back to the sanctuary and start taking confessions again until six or six-thirty. The Holy Mass would begin at seven o'clock sharp, with all the pilgrims who had arrived from Buenos Aires in the interim.

During one of these pilgrimages I met Don Ángel Fernández Artime, later rector major of the Salesians, whom I made a cardinal in the September 2023 consistory. At the time he was the principal for the Don Bosco community in Argentina. When we were introduced, he told me he came from Spain, and since then I have always called him *gallego*, or Galician, an affectionate nickname we Argentines use for all Spaniards, whether they are from Galicia or not.

To go back to the confessions: I can attest that many penitents found the answers they were seeking after coming to Luján. They would come to me in the confessional and, with a smile on their lips, tell me they at last knew how to address the situation that was tormenting them, and assure me it was the Madonna who had inspired them.

One night, a young man no more than twenty-five or twenty-six years old came to me in the confessional: tall, strong, with tattoos on his arms, earrings, long hair. I think he had lost his father. He said to me: "I've come to you because I have a big problem. After hesitating for a long time I spoke to my mother and she said, 'Make the pilgrimage to Luján; the Madonna will help, you'll see.' I was doubtful, but I listened to her and I've walked all the way here." I asked him whether he had prayed in front of the Virgin yet, and whether he had received the answer he was looking for. He replied with a smile, "I saw her, and now I know what to do." I joked, "You see, maybe I'm superfluous now." We burst out laughing, I embraced him, and he went back to his life.

Some people even went to the sanctuary during the rest of the year to ask for a miracle. I witnessed some of these with my own eyes and can tell the story of one man, a laborer, who had a very sick daughter of nearly ten. She had an infection, and the doctor said the little girl wouldn't survive the night. In tears, the man left his wife in the hospital with their daughter and caught a train to Luján. He arrived at about ten o'clock at night. The doors were closed by then, but in his desperation he spent the whole night praying outside the gate, fighting for his little girl's recovery. At six in the morning, when the doors were opened, he went in immediately and rushed to pray in front of the statue of the Madonna. Then he returned to Buenos Aires as quickly as he could. When he reached the hospital, he couldn't find his wife or daughter. He was even more desperate than before. He thought something really serious had happened, but news quickly arrived from his wife: "The doctors say our little girl is cured. Something happened; they can't explain it." You can imagine the joy of those parents, who had received a miracle, thanks to the man's nightlong battle outside the sanctuary railings, praying to the Virgin of Luján. The Lord had heard his prayer and remained by his side, watching over him and his daughter.

There is so much need for this kind of faith in this world: it is a gift to receive it, because faith as strong as this pushes human beings to fight for something. Rarely have I seen a devotion as powerful as this in the places I have visited. It is the fruit of that humble piety that arises in a particular way in Latin America, born of the encounter between the original culture of the place and the Christian faith. This too is a gift from the Lord in a world that has become secularized: it is the living God, acting on history.

This happened to me in Luján, but I had also observed it the year before, in May 2007, in Aparecida, Brazil, one of the biggest Marian shrines in the world, which attracts more than ten or eleven million pilgrims a year from all over the world. I was attending the Fifth Episcopal Conference of Latin America and the Caribbean and presided over the committee that prepared the concluding document. It truly was a moment of grace: I worked closely with Don Victor Manual Fernández, who was teaching at the Catholic University of Argentina at the time. I appointed him as prefect of the Dicastery for the Doctrine of the Faith in the summer of 2023 and made him a cardinal in September of that year. Sometimes we worked on the documents until three in the morning, and our meetings were accompanied by the songs and prayers of pilgrims entering the sanctuary. We could hear them through the window of our room. We welcomed all contributions and suggestions that reached us from the grass roots, from the people of God: I can say that the Holy Spirit was at work in that place!

The concluding document has three pillars: welcoming everything that emanates from the people; being an outward-bound, missionary church that goes out to people, to communities, to share the gift of encountering Christ the Savior; and building on the humble piety that allows us to continue to transmit the faith in a simple and authentic way. I remember the address Pope Benedict XVI gave on May 13, 2007, at the opening of our work, as if it were yesterday. He asked:

How can the Church contribute to the solution of urgent social and political problems, and respond to the great challenge of poverty and destitution? . . . Both capitalism and Marxism promised to point out the path for the creation of just structures, and they declared that these, once established, would function by themselves; they declared that not only would they have no need of any prior individual morality, but that they would promote a communal morality. And this ideological promise has been proved false. The facts have clearly demonstrated it. The Marxist system, where it found its way into government, not only left a sad heritage of economic and ecological destruction, but also a painful oppression of souls. And we can also see the same thing happening in the West, where the distance between rich and poor is growing constantly, and giving rise to a worrying degradation of personal dignity through drugs, alcohol, and deceptive illusions of happiness. . . .

Where God is absent—God with the human face of Jesus Christ—
these values fail to show themselves with their full force, nor does a
consensus arise concerning them. I do not mean that non-believers
cannot live a lofty and exemplary morality; I am only saying that
a society in which God is absent will not find the necessary consen-
sus on moral values or the strength to live according to the model of
these values, even when they are in conflict with private interests.

Prophetic words, which accompanied us all the way through the process of drafting the document, and which we were particularly able to comment on when we debated social problems and the struggle against poverty caused by the crisis. We were truly grateful to the pope for this speech. Personally, I reread it many times, as I did the Aparecida document, and it remains highly relevant to this day.

And for this reason it was a real shock to find out, on February 11, 2013, that Benedict XVI had decided to resign as pope.

XII

THE RESIGNATION
OF BENEDICT XVI

The telephone's persistent ringing echoes through the offices of the arch-diocese. It is eight o'clock in the morning, and whoever is calling knows that Cardinal Bergoglio will already be at work. After celebrating mass, however, instead of going straight down to his office, as he does nor-mally, Father Jorge has made a quick trip to Canal Orbe 21, the archdio-cese's television station, founded in 2004. Every Saturday, the channel broadcasts a program called Biblia—diálogo vigente (*Bible: Current Dialogue*), a roundtable discussion led by the protestant pastor Marcelo Figueroa, a biblical scholar and journalist, in conversation with Car-dinal Bergoglio and Abraham Skorka, rabbi of the Jewish Benei Tikva community and rector of the Latin American Rabbinical Seminary. In each episode, the three participants, who have been friends for many years, discuss, sacred texts in hand, a variety of subjects in an inter-faith ecumenical dialogue—subjects like peace, justice, faith, solitude, happiness, inclusion.

The program has become a must-watch for Catholic viewers, even though it was born almost by mistake and seemed to have few prospects *of success. It was Figueroa, in 2011, who suggested to Bergoglio that they create a space for ecumenical dialogue in the TV schedule; and the cardinal, after giving it some thought, agreed to make four pilot episodes, in the belief that television could be a good avenue for evangelism. After the first four episodes, Bergoglio endorsed the program, which had begun to focus on interfaith dialogue. Figueroa, Skorka, and Bergoglio met over meals in the synagogue and discussed the topics to be covered, while their friendship grew day by day.*

"And now it's good morning from the producer," jokes Julio Rimoldi, director general of Canal 21, greeting the seventy-six-year-old Jesuit cardinal as he does almost every day. They have known each other since the mid-1990s, when Archbishop Quarracino nominated Rimoldi as director of the diocesan radio station. As coordinator of the station he came to know Bergoglio, who was auxiliary bishop at the time, and they have kept in touch ever since.

It is the morning of February 11, 2013. The cardinal has come to the Canal 21 offices mainly to say hello to the people he works with there, but also to check on the status of the episodes yet to be broadcast and recorded. He takes the opportunity, too, to collect some DVDs given to him by the director general. Not having a television at home, Bergoglio occasionally asks the management of Canal 21 for permission to watch a movie or two that he is interested in.

"I'm sure you'll like these movies, Your Eminence," Rimoldi says confidently, handing him some DVDs that are still in their packaging.

"You know I'll come here to watch them, don't you? The player you gave me is too complicated," jokes Father Jorge as he leaves the office.

"The door is always open," Rimoldi says, walking with him toward the exit.

"Will it be open in a few months, when I retire? You do remember that I've handed in my resignation, don't you?" Father Jorge waves goodbye, laughing, and heads toward the archbishop's office with his black bag.

Señora Otilia, the cardinal's secretary, is at her desk. She has already smoked four cigarettes. She has printed out a few letters that have come into the email inbox, and now she is tidying up the list of people the cardinal will see during the course of the morning. Today is the day for the liturgical memorial of Our Lady of Lourdes, and an open-air celebration is planned for six o'clock, in front of the church dedicated to her in the Flores district, the neighborhood of Bergoglio's birth.

The telephone continues to ring in the archbishop's office. He answers it.

"Hello?"

"Your Eminence, it's Gerry. I'm calling you from Rome. I hope I'm not disturbing you. The pope has resigned."

For a moment I was paralyzed. I could hardly believe what I was hearing. This was news I had never expected to receive in my lifetime: the resignation of a pope was unimaginable, although it was provided for in canon law. In the first few moments I said to myself, "I must have misunderstood, it's not possible." But then I understood that Benedict had surely meditated and prayed for a long time before making this brave and historic decision. Faced with his declining strength, he had evidently realized that the only irreplaceable element in the Church is the Holy Spirit, and the only Lord is

Jesus Christ. This is why he was a great pope, humble and sincere, who loved the Church until the end.

The call that morning came from Gerry O'Connell, a journalist, and friend, I had known for years. He said only those words, *The pope has resigned*, and then, promising to call me back, hung up because he had a lot of work to do. Two or three hours later he called again and explained everything properly. He told me the resignation would take effect on February 28, at eight o'clock in the evening, and the conclave to elect a new pope would take place immediately after March 10.

He called me again a few days later, telling me that Benedict XVI would say farewell to the College of Cardinals on the morning of February 28, and that all cardinals would be summoned to Rome for the audience. At eight o'clock that same evening, the period of *sede vacante* (empty chair) would begin.

I must admit that over the years I had tried to go to the Vatican as little as possible: I honestly preferred being among my own people, and seeing the splendor of the Vatican buildings also made me a little uneasy. Before I knew about the audience with the cardinals, therefore, I had already booked a flight that would get me to Rome a few days before the conclave, with a return flight to Buenos Aires scheduled for March 23, the Saturday before Palm Sunday: I was sure no pope would take office during Holy Week, so I would be home in time for the Easter festival. In short, I wanted to stay in the Vatican for the minimum time necessary: my mind was focused on the celebration of Easter in Argentina and, most of all, the homilies I had to prepare for Holy Week.

When Gerry told me about Pope Benedict's meeting with the

College of Cardinals at the end of February, however, I went to the Alitalia office near the archbishop's offices to bring my departure forward to February 25. It was two o'clock in the afternoon; I went there on foot and, having taken a number, waited my turn in the waiting room. I was saying a prayer over my rosary when, about half an hour later, a stranger came up to me.

"Your Eminence, what are you doing here?" It was the manager of the ticket office.

"I came to change this ticket," I replied.

"Come into my office. I'll do it for you."

I went with him and we changed the date of my departure, and he handed me 110 dollars.

"What's this?" I asked.

"The change of flight works in your favor: the earlier one is cheaper than the one you booked. Go ahead, it's yours!"

I went back to my office to rearrange my diary: several appointments would have to be postponed until after my return from Rome. My plans included meetings, celebrations, and visits around the city; I had also scheduled some recordings of television programs. I told my friends I had to go away and also informed Marcelo Figueroa and Abraham Skorka that I would be away for some time, assuring them that we would record the episode on friendship when I came back before Easter.

I first met Marcelo in early 2000, when he was secretary general of the Argentine Bible Society; Abraham I met on the occasion of the reverences made in the cathedral twice a year at the end of the *Te Deum*, the ancient Christian hymn of thanks that in Argentina is chanted in the presence of the president on May 25, National Day, and on December 31, the end of the year. Abraham has an extremely keen mind, but he is a fan of the River Plate football team, and that certainly doesn't count in his favor. Once, in May 1999, I teased him on the subject; we were attending the usual ceremonies in the cathedral and I said to him, "I reckon we San Lorenzo fans will be eating chicken soup this year." The joke can only be understood by those who know the world of Argentine football: the River Plate team are called chickens by their opponents, because they have often lost the championship at the end of the season, despite their considerable potential. San Lorenzo was mounting a strong challenge for the championship that year, so I teased Abraham a bit, under the nose of the papal nuncio, who didn't understand a word!

Before leaving for Rome I also said goodbye to Julio Rimoldi and my collaborators at Canal 21, where I would go from time to time to watch movies on the DVDs they gave me. I still remember *Life Is Beautiful*, by Roberto Benigni; *Babette's Feast*, by Gabriel Axel; and other masterpieces of cinema. On the desk in my office, however, I left Nanni Moretti's *Habemus Papam* (We Have a Pope), which I would be sure to watch on my return; and two homilies, one for Palm Sunday and one for the Chrism Mass I would celebrate that week. But things went otherwise!

The journey was long and tiring, but I was met by friendly faces in the baggage claim area at Fiumicino airport: Cardinal Odilo Pedro Scherer, archbishop of São Paulo, considered by the press to be a candidate for the papacy, or *papabile*, was there; also Cardinal Luis Antonio Tagle, archbishop of Manila at the time, likewise included among the *papabili*, who had traveled with a compatriot of his, Cardinal Ricardo Vidal. They were all in clerical garb, except for Tagle, who was traveling in a polo shirt and jeans. I saw him again the next day and said, "There was a young man who looked just like you in the airport yesterday," and we laughed long and hard.

On the morning of February 28, I went to the Sala Clementina in the Apostolic Palace to pay my respects to Pope Benedict. Great theologian that he was, he made a very profound speech that impressed me partly because on two occasions he quoted Romano Guardini, whom I had studied at length for my doctoral dissertation. He said, quoting that theologian: "The Church is not an institution devised and built at a desk . . . but a living reality. It lives along the course of time by transforming itself, like any living being, yet its nature remains the same. At its heart is Christ."

Our applause lasted a long time. Pope Benedict took the opportunity to affirm his promise of unconditional reverence for and obedience to the new pope, who would be elected in conclave from among us. It has caused me pain over the years, however, to see how his position as pope emeritus has been exploited for ideological and political ends by unscrupulous people who have not accepted his resignation, people who may have prioritized their own interests and guarded their turf while underestimating the risk of a dramatic split within the Church.

In order to avoid damaging distractions of this kind, Benedict and I jointly decided, when I visited him at Castel Gandolfo in 2013, immediately after my election, that it would be better if he did not live out of view, as he had originally planned, but saw people and participated in the life of the Church. This decision didn't achieve much, unfortunately, because there was no shortage of disputes over the next ten years, and they harmed both sides.

During his handover to me, he gave me a white box containing the dossier, compiled by three cardinals, each over eighty years of age—Julián Herranz Casado, Jozef Tomko, and Salvatore De Giorgi—concerning the leaks of confidential documents that had shaken the Vatican in 2012. Benedict showed me the steps he had taken, removing people who were involved with lobbying groups and intervening in cases of corruption, and warned me about other situations in which it would be necessary to take action, telling me clearly that the baton was now being passed to me and it was for me to deal with it. And this I did and continue to do, following his advice.

To go back to the meeting in the Sala Clementina: I went to bid Pope Benedict farewell at the end of his speech, like all my fellow cardinals, and thanked him for everything he had done. He was very gracious and thanked me in return for having come to the audience. At precisely eight o'clock that evening, the period of *sede vacante* began: the Church no longer had a pope. The *camerlengo*, or chamberlain, Cardinal Tarcisio Bertone, sealed off the chamber that evening and, jointly with the College of Cardinals, took over the management of day-to-day affairs. The preparatory phase of the conclave was beginning, with the general congregations that we were expected to attend every day from March 4 until the morning of March 11.

The arrival of the cardinals at the Vatican is filmed by the world's media. Dressed austerely in black cassocks with colored piping, some arrive on foot, especially those who have found accommodations nearby or live in-

side the small city-state of the Vatican, while others come by car, particularly the older ones and those who live a long way away. Before going into the new Synod Hall, where the meetings are held, the cardinals greet each other and chat in front of the entrance to the building, under the curious eyes of reporters and photographers. The Americans arrive together in a coach; some Brazilians and a small group of Italians also arrive together.

Some stop to talk to the reporters; others sidestep their questions and remarks, taking refuge behind the silence imposed by the rules of the conclave. Demonstrators are protesting against the presence of certain cardinals, accused in their own dioceses of covering up cases of sexual abuse—they want them excluded from the conclave; there are also hunters of monsignorial autographs, collectors or just the curious, who will resell them online at high prices.

Cardinal Bergoglio, wrapped in his black coat, comes across St. Peter's Square alone, on foot, with his bag in his hand and without the traditional zucchetto, or skullcap, on his head. Neither the journalists nor the faithful recognize him, and this means he arrives on time, without holdups. His journey has taken about half an hour, because he has once again stayed in the Casa del Clero in Via della Scrofa, a few steps from Piazza Navona, and to reach his destination he has had to make the usual long walk.

It is March 9 by now, and for morning's general congregation the cardinal archbishop of Buenos Aires, who had been included in the list of papabili during the 2005 conclave, has written a short speech that he makes to the College of Cardinals, a statement of how the Church ought to be, in his opinion, far from self-referentiality and worldliness. He also suggests attributes to seek in the next pope.

"Cardinal Jorge Mario Bergoglio, archbishop of Buenos Aires, has asked to speak. Go ahead, Your Eminence."

Bergoglio rises to his feet, picks up the notes he has handwritten in Spanish, and starts to speak, conscious that the time available to him is limited to just three minutes: after that, the microphone will be disconnected automatically.

Good morning. We have referred to evangelizing. It is the reason for the Church's existence. "The delightful and comforting joy of evangelizing" (Paul VI). It is Jesus Christ Himself who drives us from within.

1. Evangelizing implies apostolic zeal. Evangelizing presupposes a bold willingness in the Church to come out of herself. The Church is called to come out of herself and to go to the peripheries, not only the geographical peripheries but also the existential ones: the mystery of sin, pain, injustice, ignorance, and absence of faith, all forms of deprivation, of all forms of misery.

2. When the Church does not come out of herself to evangelize, she becomes self-referential and then becomes sick—consider the woman with the stoop in the Gospel. The evils that afflict ecclesiastical institutions over time have their root in self-referentiality, in a kind of theological narcissism. In Revelation, Jesus says that He is at the door and knocks. But sometimes I think Jesus is knocking from within for us to let Him out. The self-referential Church keeps Jesus Christ within herself and does not let Him out.

3. When the Church is self-referential, she inadvertently believes she has her own light; she ceases to be the *mysterium lunae* and gives rise to that very serious evil, spiritual

worldliness—according to [Cardinal Henri] de Lubac, the worst evil that can befall the Church, living to give glory only to one another. Put simply, there are two images of the Church: the evangelizing Church that comes out of herself, the Church of *Dei verbum religiose audiens et fidente proclamans* [Listening religiously to and faithfully proclaiming the word of God] or the worldly Church that lives within herself, of herself, for herself. This should shed light on the possible changes and reforms which must be made for the salvation of souls.

4. Thinking of the next pope: a man who, through the contemplation of Jesus Christ and the adoration of Jesus Christ, helps the Church to come out of herself toward the existential peripheries, who helps her to be the fruitful mother who gains life from "the delightful and comforting joy of evangelizing."

That intervention sealed my fate! Less than three minutes that changed my life. At the end of my speech there was applause, and later I was told that my name began to circulate from that moment. I must confess that I didn't notice anything until the last day: as I said earlier, my mind was on the homilies I had left on my desk to be finished in Buenos Aires, and I couldn't wait to get back home. It was reported to me that I was spoken of a great deal during the last two days, March 12 and 13, and in fact I had even received some votes, but I thought they were what is known as provisional votes—preferences entered temporarily by electors who haven't yet decided on a candidate to vote for.

Then, on the day of my election, March 13, after spending the morning in the Sistine Chapel for the votes, I received three very clear signals.

I should explain that we were all sleeping at the Domus Sanctae Marthae, St. Martha's House, during the days of the conclave, in order to avoid any contact with the outside world. We all went back there for lunch, and before the meal I went up to the fifth floor, to the room of Cardinal Jaime Ortega y Alamino, archbishop of Havana, who had asked me for a copy of the speech I made during the general congregation. I took him the transcript, apologizing because it was handwritten and telling him I didn't have any photocopies. And he said to me, "Ah, how wonderful. I'm taking home a souvenir of the new pope." And this was the first signal, but I didn't understand that yet.

I took the elevator down to my own floor, the second, but at the fourth it stopped and Cardinal Francisco Errázuriz, archbishop emeritus of Santiago, came in. I had known him since my Aparecida days.

"Have you prepared your speech?" he asked.

"What speech?" I replied, intrigued.

"Today's—the one you'll have to make when you appear on the central loggia of the basilica," was his answer.

And that was the second signal, but I didn't understand this time either.

I went down to lunch and entered the room with Cardinal Leonardo Sandri. A few European cardinals who were already in the room said to me, "Come, Your Eminence, come over here and tell us about Latin America."

I thought nothing of it and accepted their invitation, but they gave me a thorough grilling.

At the end of the meal, as I was leaving, Cardinal Santos Abril y

Castelló, whom I had known well when he was the papal nuncio in Argentina, came up to me. He asked, "Forgive the question, Your Eminence, but is it true that you are missing a lung?"

"No, it's not true," I replied. "Only the upper lobe of my right lung is missing."

"When did this happen?" he continued.

"In 1957, when I was twenty-one," I told him.

He looked serious and remarked, in a somewhat irritated tone, "These last-minute moves!"

And that was the precise moment I realized the cardinals were thinking about me as a successor to Pope Benedict XVI.

That afternoon we went back into conclave. I found the Italian cardinal Gianfranco Ravasi in front of the Sistine Chapel, and we stopped to talk because during my studies I had always used his editions of the sapiential, or poetic, books of the Bible, particularly the book of Job. We stayed outside, comparing notes as we walked up and down near the entrance. It was as if, after my conversations at lunchtime, at some subconscious level I didn't want to go in, for fear I would be elected. Eventually, one of the pontifical masters of ceremonies came out and said, "Are you going in or not?"

I was nearly elected on the first ballot, and at that stage the Brazilian cardinal Cláudio Hummes approached me and said, "Don't be afraid! This is how the Holy Spirit works." And then, on the third ballot of the afternoon, when the seventy-seventh vote was counted and my name had received two-thirds of the electors' votes, everyone applauded for a long time. While the ballot papers were being scrutinized, Hummes came over to me again, kissed me, and said the words that have stayed in my heart and mind ever since: "Don't forget the poor."

And there and then I chose the name I would have as pope: Francis, in honor of St. Francis of Assisi. I formally communicated this to Cardinal Giovanni Battista Re. The dean, Cardinal Angelo Sodano, and the vice dean, Cardinal Roger Etchegaray, were not present at the conclave because they were over eighty, so Re, as the senior cardinal bishop in attendance, assumed the responsibilities of the dean in the Sistine Chapel, as prescribed by the rules. It was he who asked me the two questions laid down in the procedure: "Do you accept your canonical election as supreme pontiff?" and "By what name do you wish to be called?"

My life had once again been thrown into turmoil by God's plan. The Lord was at my side: I could feel Him. He was expecting me, and He was walking with me during this new responsibility in the service of the Church and the faithful, as decided by the cardinals, whose actions were guided by the Holy Spirit.

When the moment came for me to don the vestments of a pope for the first time, in the Sistine Chapel's so-called Room of Tears, the master of the Office for the Liturgical Celebrations of the Supreme Pontiff, Monsignor Guido Marini, was with me and patiently explained everything that needed to be done. He showed me the pectoral cross, the red shoes, the cassock in three sizes, and other papal accessories including the short red cape, or *mozzetta*. I said to him, "Thank you for your work, monsignore, but I'm very fond of my own things. I'll just wear the white cassock, and I'll keep my archbishop's pectoral cross and my shoes—which are orthopedic!" He was very accommodating, and accepted my decision. I told the master of ceremonies I wanted Cardinal Hummes and the then–cardinal vicar of the Diocese of Rome, Agostino Vallini, beside me in the central loggia of the basilica after the *Habemus papam* announcement. And my wish was respected.

I cannot deny that I felt very emotional when I saw all those people in St. Peter's Square, waiting to see the new pope. There were flags from all over the world, prayers, songs, and despite the rain everyone had stayed and waited. The Spirit breathed on the people; it was a moment of grace for the whole Church, and a single chorus of prayers rose up to the heavens, giving thanks to the Lord.

I thought of my parents, Grandma Rosa, my brothers and sisters; I thought of all the poor, discarded people I had known throughout my life and found the strength to remember them, deciding to put them at the center of my service. A poor Church for the poor, a field-hospital Church, an outward-bound, missionary Church, with a reformed curia in Rome, as requested by the College of Cardinals.

Having been greeted by the people, my first telephone call was to Benedict, now pope emeritus. I wanted to thank him once again for his work, asking him to pray for me and promising to go and see him very soon. When the time came for dinner, I called the papal nuncio in Argentina, Archbishop Emil Paul Tscherrig, whom I made a cardinal in the September 2023 consistory. I told him to instruct the bishops and local clergy not to come to my inaugural mass on March 19, and to donate to the poor the money they would have spent on flights.

The following morning I donned my white cassock for the second time, but I had some difficulties with the collar. My neighbor across the corridor was Cardinal Paolo Romeo, archbishop of Palermo. Fortunately, he happened to be in the corridor and gave me a hand putting it on. After morning mass and breakfast, I went to the Basilica of Santa Maria Maggiore to pray before the image of the Madonna *Salus populi romani* (Salvation of the Roman people) and entrust my papacy to her. And since I was outside the Vatican, I went over to the residence in Via della Scrofa to pick up my few belongings there and pay the bill that was still pending.

In the afternoon, after mass in the Sistine Chapel, I was taken to see the papal apartment on the third level of the Apostolic Palace, but I thought it was too grand for me: if I had stayed in that historic residence of popes, I'm sure I would have needed the services of a psychiatrist! I need to be among people to feel well; there, I would have been somewhat isolated from the outside world. Saint Martha's House was the ideal solution: on the floor where I had stayed during the conclave there was a slightly larger room that was usually set aside for the pope-elect. I was shown this room, and I moved in as soon as it was ready. There is a small reception room for visitors, a bedroom with a bathroom and a small office, and another bathroom for visitors.

I have tried to keep up the habits I had in Buenos Aires, trying not to unsettle my life too much. One of the things I have certainly missed most, especially during the early years, is the ability to go out into the streets, to go and help the poor on the outskirts of the city, to use public transport to move around, to go and have a pizza with friends, as I used to in Argentina. In compensation, though, I have met good people I didn't know before, and for this I thank the Lord every day. I talk often to my family, my sister, my cousins, and my old friends—phone calls, letters, and emails. We don't make video calls because I can't manage them, but we keep in touch by traditional means. Many lifelong friends are no longer with us, sadly, but I think of them always and pray for them.

As far as my service is concerned, there is no shortage of plans: there are still so many things to do. During these years the Lord has given me the gift of experiencing moments of great joy. I am thinking of the simplest things (like an encounter or a handshake), but also the most important—for example, the traveling I have done all over the world, and the people I have had the chance to embrace in the Americas, Africa, and Asia.

I am thinking of my first trip to the island of Lampedusa, in the Mediterranean Sea, the landing point and gateway to Europe for people desperately seeking a future far from famine and war. After a massive loss of life in the Mediterranean shortly before my visit, I felt it my duty in July 2013 to accept an invitation from the parish priest of that particular periphery, Don Stefano Nastasi, and begin my own journey, retracing the migrants' route, which is not finished yet because there is still so much work to be done on the subject of migration.

In my own country, Argentina, the new president, Javier Milei, has invited me to undertake a journey of "pacification" there. The situation is not simple: so many people are suffering poverty, and I want to convey my closeness to them. I hope I will manage to go; I would like to, although it's not as easy for me to travel as it used to be, especially over long distances. We shall see what the Lord decides for me.

I think, too, about the dialogue and forward steps made with our Jewish brothers, our Orthodox brothers, on a very fruitful ecumenical journey in fraternal dialogue, as well as the edifying dialogue with our Muslim brothers.

I think of the forward steps made by the Church in recent years: a Church on a journey, a Church that listens as only a mother can; a synodal Church, united, that places itself at the service of the people of God, even though there are those within it, consumed by pride and egotism and prey to diabolical temptations, who would like to see it divided as if there were two groups of rival fans.

Then I think of women, who are finding more and more space and attention within the Church's structures. I think of the laity and the young, who are great treasures and a great hope for the future.

But in recent years we have also experienced, and continue to experience, some very painful tests. I am thinking of the dispersed Third World War that has been convulsing the world for too long: conflicts in various parts of the planet that are destroying humanity and the sense of community between peoples, with more and more of our brothers and sisters suffering beneath the bombs. To those who have no pity or remorse for the poor souls who are dying I make yet another appeal: Stop the weapons! Stop the bombs! Stop the thirst for power! Stop, in the name of God! Enough, I beg you!

I think of the ever-intensifying exploitation of our shared home, the earth. The question of the environment cannot be postponed any longer; it has become so urgent, so dramatic, that I made the decision to attend the United Nations Climate Change Conference, COP28, in Dubai, in the United Arab Emirates, in late November and early December 2023. Unfortunately, a pulmonary infection obliged me to stay at home: my doctors advised me against making things worse by undertaking the journey and suffering the extremes of temperature I could expect in that country. To be clear: I was inclined to go anyway, somewhat reckless as I am, to spur the world's leaders to change course. And change course we must, or it will be the end of everything, and all the sacrifices that have been made over so many years will have been in vain.

In the end, though, I followed the doctors' advice and entrusted my speech to Cardinal Pietro Parolin, the Vatican's secretary of state, who gave it on December 2. What we are doing to creation, he said on my behalf, is a grave offense to God. And I'd like to add that it is a grave betrayal of the weakest among us, who will suffer the consequences more than anyone. Consider, for example, the climate refugees fleeing lands that have been devastated by drought, or populations struck by disastrous floods, storms, and other weather-related phenomena. The planet's screaming can no longer be ignored: there is no more time, we are gambling with the future of the young, with the future of humanity itself.

And finally, I think of the tragic years during which we experienced the COVID-19 pandemic, a moment that has made us realize how fragile the world is, and how humanity needs to stop and look in the mirror to think about itself anew.

XIII

THE COVID-19 PANDEMIC

Solitude has settled on the center of Rome. A ghostly silence reigns: gone are the clamor around the Colosseum, the guitars strumming in front of the Pantheon; the alleyways of Trastevere are deserted, the restaurant shutters are down, even though it's Sunday. The street musicians have vanished with their accordions, along with the peddlers around the Vatican. Saint Peter's Square, normally crowded with thousands of worshippers attending the pope's Angelus, is completely empty at midday: Pope Francis did not appear at the window. He said the Marian prayer indoors, recorded by television cameras inside the private library of the Apostolic Palace, so that it could be followed only on television, on the radio, or via the internet.

The last of the tourists who used to line up to visit the basilica or the Vatican museums have managed to get away before the infection could reach them, and now only seagulls make their presence felt as they scavenge among the overflowing garbage containers. The only citizens circulating in Rome are in the hospitals and pharmacies, or lining up outside supermarkets; they wait their turn to enter and try to obtain some of life's necessities—flour, milk, pasta, yeast, water, oil—hoping the shelves will not be empty.

On this afternoon, March 15, 2020, football fans' radios are not tuned to matches: the stadiums are closed, the championship has been suspended. The airwaves play only music and news bulletins enumerating the dead: fourteen hundred in Italy, said yesterday's six p.m. bulletin from the Department of Civil Protection, with more than twenty thousand infected since the beginning of the pandemic. Intensive-care units are on the verge of collapse, particularly in the north; nursing homes are like powder kegs, ready to explode. Italy is experiencing the nightmare of the COVID-19 pandemic, caused by a coronavirus that was first identified in China and spread like an oil slick around the world, from the United States to New Zealand.

A few days before, on March 9, the Italian government, in an announcement from the prime minister, ordered a state of lockdown across the country: no one is allowed to leave their home except in cases of emergency; most businesses must stay closed to avoid gatherings, as must schools, churches, gyms, museums, cinemas, and theaters. "Stay at home" is the order, recorded on tape and broadcast from megaphones on police cars as they drive around the streets.

Pope Francis has been attentively following the worldwide development of the pandemic for weeks, reading reports from the World Health Organization that are delivered to him almost every day. He prays for the victims and their families, for those whose lives have been turned upside down, for those who have lost their jobs, for old people who have been left alone. But he feels he must do something more to stop this tiny and invisible foe.

And so, on that cold Sunday afternoon, enveloped in the silence of a Rome that seems to be asleep, the man in white decides, after a short journey by car, to go for a walk in the deserted streets. He is alone, apart from the men of the Vatican Corps of Gendarmerie accompanying him at a discreet distance. Pope Francis made a surprise departure from the Vatican, a little after four in the afternoon, for a pilgrimage in two stages, to the Basilica of Santa Maria Maggiore and to the Church of San Marcello al Corso. The first houses the icon of the Madonna known as Salus populi romani, *or Salvation of the Roman People, to whom Francis has entrusted his papacy. The second houses a fourteenth-century wooden crucifix, known as the miraculous crucifix, that survived intact when a fire destroyed the church overnight in May 1519. Three years later, in the summer of 1522, when Rome was hit by an outbreak of plague, the great crucifix was lifted shoulder-high and carried in procession through the* rioni, *or quarters, of the capital to St. Peter's Square. The faithful repeated this ritual every day for the next sixteen days, almost to the end of August, until the epidemic came to an end.*

I had been reflecting for some time, during the early days of the pandemic, pondering what gesture I could make. Faced with the dramatic state of affairs in Italy and the rest of the world, I decided to visit the crucified Christ and the Madonna *Salus populi romani*. I pay a visit to the Madonna every time I go on an apostolic journey, when I come back, and in many other situations.

I warned the gendarmerie that I would be going out for an important engagement that afternoon, so once we had driven about as far as Piazza Venezia, I set off on foot along Via del Corso toward the Church of San Marcello, where the miraculous crucifix I had heard so much about was preserved. It was incredible: I was in the heart of Rome at four-thirty on a Sunday afternoon, and I was completely surrounded by silence. There was nobody around: no taxis, no tourist coaches, not a single passerby. The setting was as unreal as it was dramatic, and I thought of all those people forced to stay indoors to avoid contagion. In the past, when I was a cardinal, I had done a lot of walking on these Roman streets, and even as pope I had gone into the center from time to time, to see the optician or visit a store or two; and the traffic was always a presence, like the tourists and the Romans, at all hours of the day and night. Perhaps this is why I was so struck, that Sunday afternoon, by the silence and desolation that blanketed the whole city.

During that short journey on foot I prayed hard to the Lord, thinking of the victims of the virus, but also the health workers and volunteers. I prayed for the priests and nuns who had been infected in hospital wards and had died; I prayed that government officials might find solutions soon.

Once inside the church, with some flowers to lay at the foot of the crucifix in its protective cabinet, I was greeted by a group of ten friars, and we spent several minutes standing in silence before Christ on the cross. I spoke to Him from the heart, with the familiarity that exists between brothers or friends. I appealed for an end to the pandemic and asked Him to remember us all, and not to abandon us during this ordeal for all humanity.

That same morning, before the Angelus—which, sadly, I had recited indoors—I had made a point of thanking the clergy for their apostolic zeal and their creativity: because priests had found a thousand ways to be close to their people, particularly in Lombardy, in northern Italy, which had been hit particularly hard in the early days of the pandemic, so they wouldn't feel abandoned.

One fine bishop, an Italian, had telephoned me during that time. He was going through a difficult time because of the number of cases of COVID-19 and patients in the hospital in his diocese. He told me with sadness that he was visiting all the hospitals during the week, including Sundays, to bless and grant absolution to the sick, but that he did this from the waiting room because he wasn't allowed into the intensive care unit, where he would face the risk of contagion. He had been criticized for this by certain experts in canon law, who had said that absolution was permitted only when there was direct physical contact. He asked me, "What can I do?" I answered simply that he should carry out his duty as a priest and act as the Lord would wish. He thanked me, and later I was told he had continued to grant absolutions.

This and others are examples of great compassion, of love for the people, from priests who do not give in to cowardice—like Don Abbondio in Alessandro Manzoni's 1827 novel *The Betrothed*—but who put people first, sometimes at the risk of their own lives. And since I mention Manzoni's masterpiece, I am also reminded of Cardinal Federico Borromeo, whom I have called a hero of the Great Plague of Milan in the seventeenth century. In his *De pestilentia*, which Manzoni used as an historical source when he was writing his novel, the cardinal writes that he would move around the stricken city in a sedan chair, protected behind glass, and would wave through the windows rather than going near anyone. This hiding behind glass seems not to have been popular with the people: they wanted the proximity and comfort of their pastor. During COVID-19, however, many priests were close to their parishioners, and I also recall the nurses and doctors who neglected their own families every day to be beside the sick.

I would have liked to play my part with some more concrete gestures. How I would have liked to visit hospitals to give comfort to sick people left alone! How I would have liked to visit nursing homes and listen to the stories of elderly people who had been through months of isolation! How I would have liked to say a rosary with all the people who had been locked inside their homes for months, unable to go out! But the health restrictions obliged me to stay penned up indoors, forced to change my habits, and I cannot deny it: I suffered greatly. Fortunately, I stayed in contact with everyone through social media: we held many meetings online, and I celebrated mass in the small chapel at St. Martha's House, asking for it to be broadcast on television and the internet so that everyone could unite in prayer.

This period of lockdown-induced solitude also helped to deliver me from the temptation to selfishness, because I had the opportunity to pray more and think more about other people. In addition, I thought hard about how to handle my role as bishop of Rome once the crisis had passed.

During those months I proceeded with one certainty: we would all emerge from this test as either better or worse people. The only way to emerge as a better person would be to carry out a review of everything, analyzing the most dramatic situations and taking them on board with realism. Indeed, it is only possible to face crises with realism. Consider, for example, the fact that everything stopped during the COVID-19 pandemic and, at the environmental level, it was as if the planet had started to breathe again. Seems contradictory, doesn't it? But in fact there is a Spanish proverb that says, "God always forgives; we do, sometimes; nature, never." And that's exactly what happened: distracted by other priorities, we didn't pay attention to catastrophes as they arrived, and they blew up before we noticed them. Let us not forget that everything is interconnected, and that our health depends on that of the ecosystems created by God. Coronavirus, like the melting of the glaciers or the tremendous wildfires that destroy vast areas of vegetation, may be a reaction from nature to the neglect and exploitation brought about by us humans.

We can certainly say that a way of life has been prevalent until now that ruthlessly destroys the environment. What has been lacking is contemplation, and this has given way to an arrogant anthropocentricity that has led humankind to believe it has absolute dominion over all creatures. Whereas instead, it is our duty, alongside the generations that will come after us, to be custodians of our common home, to rebuild what we have destroyed, and to correct everything that wasn't working, even before COVID-19, and that played its part in making the crisis worse.

I am delighted to see how young people, especially schoolchildren, are already committed to fighting for the protection of the environment, protesting against the decisions of governments that don't intervene sufficiently regarding climate change. Time is almost up: we don't have much time to save the planet, and when I think of those young men and women going out into the streets, I always say they are *haciendo lío*, making a lot of noise, which is a good thing, provided their protest marches don't descend into violence and don't end up defacing public spaces or works of art.

Rich or poor, we are all involved in this crisis, and sadly I must state that during the period of the pandemic a few political personalities displayed hypocrisy—on the one hand saying they wanted to address the crisis and fight world hunger, while on the other hand spending a fortune on weapons. We need cohesion; we need a rebirth to blow the wind of trust into the citizenry.

And I would like to add that it is also necessary to pray more. People pray too little in this fluid society, bewildered by the speed of events that allow no time for a moment's reflection. People pray too little in their families: the evening prayers in their native language or in dialect, the ones taught to us by our grandmothers, are increasingly being forgotten, and many people have moved away from faith because they think the pandemic was a divine punishment. Not true! The Lord loves human beings; the Lord is the Lord of life, not of death! This is why, at the most difficult time during lockdown, I wanted to guide an extraordinary moment of prayer in St. Peter's Square, one that involved the whole world.

"We're ready to go, Your Holiness, when you're ready."

Pope Francis nods. "Yes, I'm coming."

A valet has knocked at the door to warn him that the appointed time is near. The eighty-three-year-old pontiff, absorbed in reading the gospel in his office at St. Martha's House, with a small lamp illuminating his desk, is making a few changes to the text of the meditation he is about to present. He has worked hard on it, searching for the right words to communicate his state of mind, and at the same time instill confidence in his listeners. His staff are waiting for him, umbrellas open, at the entrance; the car is on its way. It will take him under the Arco delle Campane, the official entrance to the Vatican, and up to the foot of the fanlike steps leading to the platform in front of the sanctuary in St. Peter's Square. The huge statues of the apostles Peter and Paul, accustomed to watching over pilgrims arriving from all over the planet, are wrapped in a surreal silence.

The square is forlorn, bereft of its usual fervor, and the surrounding air exudes a mixture of fear and despair. To make the moment even more theatrical, imagine the driving rain of a slow-moving storm that has engulfed the city, even though it is spring, and is lighting up the gloomy late March sky with bolts of lightning. In the background, the only sound is the wailing of sirens as ambulances go back and forth between hospitals and the homes of people who have been struck down by disease. The number of dead is rising day by day, and there are now nearly ninety thousand cases of COVID-19 in Italy. People cling to whatever they can, seizing on every solution that comes to their attention, even the most unlikely. All over the world, they are weeping for victims; there seems to be no way out, nothing that might overcome this invisible enemy, which by this point has spread to every corner of the globe, forcing nations to shut the door on social relations. But there is one light of hope that still burns: that of faith, that of whoever prays to God to put an end to this torment.

The car has arrived in St. Peter's Square with the pope on board, and Francis has gotten out to walk toward the platform that has been prepared at the top of the steps leading up to the main entrance to the sanctuary. His steps are the slow and lonely steps of a pastor who is *bearing the hopes and fears of the world on his shoulders, the steps of Jorge Mario Bergoglio the man. He looks up at two huge symbols of hope in the sanctuary: the miraculous crucifix from the Church of San Marcello al Corso and the icon of the* Salus populi romani. *He wanted them here beside him for his* Statio orbis *address on March 27, 2020, for this unique moment of spiritual unity, of collective communion despite physical separation.*

Francis gathers himself in prayer; beside him, the master of the Office for the Liturgical Celebrations of the Supreme Pontiff assists him, reading a passage from the gospel. Then the pope starts calmly and reassuringly reading out his meditation: his words echo across the deserted piazza, but they reach the hearts of billions of people. His speech dissolves in the silence, but those at home join with him in spirit, confident that they are no longer alone on this long and arduous journey, certain that the presence of the pastor, there in the piazza in the rain, will accompany them through the storm. Francis looks into the distance toward the silent city. His eyes are glistening. Then he looks to his right, toward the prominent monument to migrants from various historical periods, men and women crammed together in a small boat. Francis reads:

> For weeks now it has been evening. Thick darkness has gathered over our squares, our streets, and our cities; it has taken over our lives, filling everything with a deafening silence and a distressing void that stops everything as it passes by; we feel it in the air, we notice it in people's gestures, their glances give them away. We find ourselves afraid and lost. Like the disciples in the Gospel we were

caught off guard by an unexpected, turbulent storm. We have realized that we are on the same boat, all of us fragile and disoriented, but at the same time important and needed, all of us called to row together, each of us in need of comforting the other. On this boat . . . are all of us. Just like those disciples, who spoke anxiously with one voice, saying "We are perishing," so we too have realized that we cannot go on thinking of ourselves, but only together can we do this.

Faith and hope were stronger at that moment than any virus. The world had fallen victim to darkness, and so I thought a moment of prayer was needed, to bring everyone together and feed the flame of hope that would light a path for the world. The idea for this extraordinary prayer in St. Peter's Square came from a priest, Don Marco Pozza, chaplain of a prison in northern Italy, who had made the suggestion of a *Statio orbis* to me, a strong gesture that might unite the people of the entire planet in a single chorus toward the heavens. It was an extraordinary moment, because I had never found myself in that situation in the square, which is normally crowded with worshippers.

Many have wondered what I was thinking about as I walked toward the sanctuary. It was nothing remarkable; I was just thinking about people's loneliness. I was alone, and many people were living in the same situation as me, though certainly in more difficult conditions. As I walked, I had a thought that I would define as inclusive, because my heart and my mind were with every human being: I was completely with you.

It is true that I was alone in the square, but only physically, because spiritually I was in contact with people everywhere, and I felt that proximity in the strength of prayer, the prayer that works miracles. This is why I asked for the miraculous crucifix and the *Salus populi romani* to be present too. I stopped in prayer before Christ on the cross and asked Him to intervene in the pandemic. I used an expression we often use in Argentina: *meté mano, por favor*—"play your part, please." I went on: "You resolved a situation like this in the 1500s; you know what to do." I was clinging to prayer myself, looking for a miracle, and I did the same before the icon of the Madonna, entrusting the world to her and asking her to be mother not just to the Roman people but to the whole planet.

From the heights of the sanctuary I looked out at the utterly empty square. Silence reigned: all you could hear were sirens and the ever-strengthening rain. Despite the absence of people, I felt we were together, although distanced. Then I looked at the monument with the boatload of migrants in the distance and thought about the boat we were all in, fearful, not knowing how many of us would still be here by the end of the journey.

It was a powerful moment. Grief could easily have won the day, but I found a ray of hope when, at the end, before the eucharistic adoration, I kissed Jesus's feet on the crucifix. Christ is truly the redemption of humanity.

The moment with the greatest meaning came when I held in my hands the Blessed Sacrament for the *Urbi et orbi* blessing: I entrusted my diocese, Rome, and the world to the Lord, imploring Him to put an end to the tragedy. In the prayer I remembered principally the victims' families and the people working on the front lines, but also families feeling the weight of the crisis triggered by all the restrictions; people with serious disabilities; people on the fringes of society, who seemed to have been forgotten by everyone; people living on the street, exposed to the virus with no means of protection against it; children who weren't allowed out of the house; people without relatives, sometimes far from home, who couldn't meet anyone at all; migrants and undocumented people in general; the incarcerated. But also everyone who had been unable to say goodbye to their loved ones in a shared funeral ceremony.

This grim scenario began to change with the arrival of the first vaccines. Deciding whether to get vaccinated is always an ethical choice, but I know that many people signed up to movements opposed to the administration of the medication. This distressed me because in my view, being against the antidote is an almost suicidal act of denial.

There were even a few anti-vaxxers among the bishops: some came close to death. I believe a generalized fear was created when superficial explanations of how the vaccines worked spoke of injections of the virus into the body. There were also claims there was nothing but water in the vials; some people even stated publicly that microchips were being implanted in people. All this created confusion and panic. When the first supplies arrived at the Vatican, I scheduled my vaccination immediately; later I got the boosters as well, and, thanks be to God, I have not caught the virus.

But I suffered during that time too, because I couldn't shake hands with the faithful, couldn't stroke the faces of children or old people, couldn't embrace anyone who asked for a gesture of closeness. And I suffered because I had to cancel or postpone a number of projects and trips. Many people—particularly poor people—knocked insistently at my door, asking for the vaccine, and eventually, by agreement with the papal almoner, Cardinal Konrad Krajewski, we organized vaccinations for the homeless, who of course didn't have the papers necessary to prove their residence, as required, at other vaccination centers. There was a great wave of voluntary assistance, not just in Rome but all over the world.

Although at first we all felt as if we were in the same boat, brothers and sisters together, I must recognize that after a while the temptation to revert to "every man for himself" took over. This distracted attention from the most serious situations in favor of focusing on the self, the *I*, and relegating the *we*, the spirit of community, to second place. Let us consider, for example, the attention paid to the poor seeking help to get vaccinated or to be treated for the disease: it was as if their voices had been silenced. Their stories and their faces were moving, of course, but during periods of restrictions—which for some people led to a great fear of physical contact—the presence of a poor, homeless, or disadvantaged person was irritating and created a new level of marginalization. Fortunately, there were many good Samaritans, good Christians who took care of the most vulnerable, not only during lockdowns but also during the whole period of the pandemic. God intervened so that these people might leave the door open, despite the crisis, without giving way to anger and fear.

And so, gradually, we got back on our feet, the world regained its confidence; even we of the Vatican were able to go back to all our activities, audiences, and in-person celebrations, with the basilica once again crowded with people. I went back to traveling and meeting friends and worshippers, although during the months and years that followed, I did experience illness, not because of the coronavirus, and received treatment in the hospital.

This too was a powerful experience, because sickness in us Christians can inspire growth and understanding of the things that truly matter in life. And it also gives us the opportunity to experience human, Christian solidarity to the full, in God's way: closeness, compassion, tenderness. On the hospital wards I met many sick people who were fighting for their lives, especially young people, and it touched my heart. Many times I asked myself, echoing Ivan in Dostoevsky's *The Brothers Karamazov*, "Why do children suffer?" It is a question that cannot receive a human answer. The best answers we can give are prayer and service to them.

On the subject of children: in the Vatican we are still suffering greatly from the disappearance, more than forty years ago, of one of our citizens, Emanuela Orlandi, who was fifteen years old at the time. I continue to pray for her and her family, particularly her mother. An inquiry has been opened at the Vatican, in order to shed light on the story and bring out the truth. As far as Emanuela is concerned, though, I would like every family that is mourning the loss of one of their own to feel my closeness. I am at their side.

My medical treatments gave me plenty to reflect on, but in the meantime others were more interested in politics, in campaigning for votes, almost considering a new conclave. Relax, it's human, there's nothing shocking about it. When the pope is in the hospital, there are many things to think about, and some people will speculate for their own purposes or to earn some money from the press. Fortunately, I have never thought of resigning, despite moments of difficulty, but I will talk about that soon.

Thanks to the Lord's help and the prayers of so many of the faithful, I have carried on, finding myself now confronted by other humanitarian emergencies, other global crises: first, the war in Ukraine that has convulsed Europe, the great conflict that has steeped that country in blood; and then, since October 2023, a new conflict in the Middle East. I have asked, and continue to ask, day after day, for the world's wars to come to an end, for dialogue to prevail, for attention to be paid to caring for children and the elderly, who are suffering, for the anguish of families over their kidnapped loved ones to be considered. Even I have lost a few friends from Argentina in the bombing of Gaza—very painful—people I have known for years, who suddenly lost their lives at the hands of human beings. And I have felt great sorrow hearing the daily count of victims, and learning of battles inside hospitals.

To make my presence known, every day I have called the parish priest of Gaza, who is of Argentine origin, and also some of the nuns working among the population. And on two separate occasions I have had meetings in the Vatican with relatives of Israeli hostages and relatives of Palestinians who were stuck in Gaza as it was being bombed. I can assure you that there was no difference between them. Their expressions were the same: simple people in need of love. There was no desire for vengeance in those eyes; there was just the desire to find the silence of peace and serene coexistence, without threats and without weapons. Only in this way can there be a future for this wounded humanity.

XIV

A HISTORY YET
TO BE WRITTEN

For hours, a member of the Swiss Guard has been standing motionless in the corridor outside the small apartment not far from the elevator on the second floor of St. Martha's House. In the background, the hum of a fan can be heard; voices are hushed, to avoid any disturbance; people come and go in front of the pope's room, walking as quietly as possible. The young man, about twenty years old and well over six feet tall, watches people as they go in and out, gives a military salute, smiles at the occasional joke. His uniform, Renaissance in style, looks like something from a painting by Raphael. Legend has it that it was designed by Michelangelo but that is just a story which has been handed down over the decades; in fact, it was the brainchild of a certain Commander Jules Repond, taking inspiration from Rafael's frescoes in the early 1900s, when nobody imagined that the twentieth century would be thrown into turmoil by two world wars and many other events that have been seared into the collective memory.

"Are you still alive?"

Pope Francis has come out into the corridor. He is on his way to the room where the multilingual collection of books and other publications to be given to visitors is kept. He needs to find a particular volume containing his speeches on Europe, because he plans to give it as a gift to the person who is about to arrive. It is probably the sixth time since morning that the eighty-seven-year-old pontiff has encountered the guard outside his room, and it is now three fifteen on a chilly winter afternoon. A friendly joke that catches the young man off guard, but raises a smile.

"Er, yes, Your Holiness. I'm definitely alive," the guard replies, saluting and breaking the silence that historically has surrounded the papal presence.

"Have you eaten today?" asks the pope.

And the halberdier smiles again, nodding his thanks.

Before going into the book room, the pope places a paper note under the statuette of the sleeping St. Joseph, checks the box for incoming mail, and leaves a few sheets in the outbox. He also takes a handful of filled chocolates brought to him by some Brazilian bishops—typical desserts from the Amazon, they had told him. He'll give some to his guest, who has now arrived in the hall of the residence. On the ground floor priests and laypeople silently come and go, while Swiss guards in plain clothes (black suits) and the men of the Vatican gendarmerie check that everything is in order; a Swiss guard with an earpiece escorts the visitor into the salon, where the pope will soon arrive.

"Wait here, please," he says firmly, with a marked German accent.

Meanwhile, on the second floor, the pontiff is entering the office-turned-library, which is filled with the scent of both yellowing pages and freshly printed volumes. Confidently, he heads toward the shelf that houses multiple copies of the book he wants to take to his meeting.

"Your guest has arrived, Your Holiness," a valet informs him.

"Yes, thank you," he replies, putting the book into a bag that already contains two other publications, some rosary beads, and the Brazilian chocolates.

A few moments later, he reaches the hall using the elevator. The Swiss guard in front of his room has radioed a coded message to his colleagues on the ground floor, telling them the pontiff is heading for their part of the domus. Francis allows some passing guests to take selfies with him, then knocks quickly on the door and goes into the salon with a smile, where his guest is waiting for him. An enormous picture of Mary, Untier of Knots, hangs on the wall.

"How are you? Take your jacket off if you like, no need to be formal, eh?" the pontiff says to his guest, immediately putting him at ease. With a gesture, he offers the man a seat in one of the armchairs. A couple of jokes, a moment of prayer, and a chat that touches on subjects ranging from war to sports and interfaith dialogue, and finally a reflection on the role to be played by the Catholic Church in the immediate future, and how society will change in the years to come. In that salon, the power and grandeur of this figure, the spiritual leader of the Catholic world, yield to the simple humanity that transforms him into a priest listening to a believer.

"Do you know what someone has written about you, Holy Father?" his guest begins after about half an hour of conversation. "That you are destroying the image of the papacy, because you have eliminated the distance between it and the people."

Francis smiles, says nothing for a few moments, looks up, and then meets his visitor's gaze.

Yes, I kept quiet for a moment, thinking that if I looked into everything that was said and written about me, I wouldn't have time to do anything else, and I would need a weekly session with a psychologist! But as it happened I had read that particular statement somewhere: "Francis is destroying the papacy." And what can I say today? That my vocation is to be a priest: above all else I am a priest. I am a pastor, and a pastor must be among his people, talk to them, enter into dialogue, listen, support them, watch over them.

Today it is no longer right to create distances. Jesus did not place Himself above His people; He was of the people and walked among them. It's true that the Vatican is the last absolute monarchy in Europe, and that courtly arguments and maneuvers are often seen there, but such scheming needs to be defeated and abandoned once and for all.

Fortunately, the demand for reform of this kind came from the majority of cardinals present at the general congregations in 2013. There was a strong desire to change things, to abandon certain attitudes, which, sadly, have proved difficult to eradicate. Needless to say, there are always some who wish to put the brakes on reform, who want things always to stay as they were during the days of pope kings, who dream of superficial change that preserves the status quo, and this is certainly not good for the Church. And speaking of the conclave: some American media outlets had reported that I intended to change the rules to give nuns and the laity a vote in the election of the new pope. But this was fantasy, obviously invented and circulated to create bad feeling within the Church and disorientation among the faithful.

But I still cultivate a dream for the future: that our Church might be a meek, humble, servant church, with all the attributes of God—therefore also tender, close, and compassionate. We must proceed with much that is new, many projects: for example, the Jubilee in

2025, which will inspire a great surge in faith, besides being an opportunity to rediscover a climate of hope.

We must always face the horizon with confidence, especially when it comes to the countries and continents where vocations are flourishing and there is a thirst for the Lord, places where there is a thirst for closeness and listeners and the Church is seen as an oasis where that thirst may be slaked. In this context, some have suggested a return to the Church as it was at its beginnings, that of the first Christian communities, but this is just a romantic image: we must simplify things as we look to the future, overcome clericalism, that is, the view of clerics as an elite with an attitude of moral superiority over and distance from the faithful. It has become a disease, a plague! The Church is full of saints, but in some cases it has become a corrupt Church, precisely because clericalism is corrupt.

When I think about the Church to come, I am reminded of Joseph Ratzinger's theory. He spoke of a Church that will move forward but in a different way: it will be a smaller, more distinctive institution. It was 1969, and the Bavarian theologian traced his own vision of the future in a cycle of radio lessons, saying that what awaited us was a Church that would start afresh from a position of minority status, with few adherents, placing faith at the center of all experience; a more spiritual, poorer Church that would become a home for the indigent, for those who have not lost sight of God.

During the years of theological debate after the closing message of the Second Vatican Council, Ratzinger was talking about a crucial time for human beings, an historical moment that made the period between medieval and modern times seem insignificant. At the time, there were hints of an attempt to turn priests into something like functionaries, social workers, relevant politically but not spiritually. For this reason, too, we must fight the scourge of clericalism: it is a perversion that may destroy the Church, because instead of promoting laypeople, it kills them by exercising power over them.

It is no coincidence that Don Primo Mazzolari, in his writings, gave a warning about priests who, rather than offering sustenance and warmth to the hearts of their brothers and sisters, suffocate all signs of life in them. But the virus of clericalism can also infect the laity. This is terrible, because these are people who ask to be clericalized but stay on the margins of decision-making so as not to take responsibility. It is the opposite of synodality, where the people of God converge on and actively participate in the path of the Church.

In this context I imagine a mother Church, who embraces and welcomes everyone, even those who feel they are in the wrong and have been judged by us in the past. I think, for example, of homosexuals and transsexuals who seek the Lord but are rejected or persecuted. Many have spoken of *Fiducia supplicans*, the statement from the Dicastery for the Doctrine of the Faith on the blessing of couples in irregular situations. I just want to say that God loves everyone, especially sinners. And if my brother bishops, according to their discernment, decide not to follow this path it doesn't mean that this is the antechamber to schism, because the Church's doctrine is not brought into question. Even in the synod on synodality, due to conclude in October 2024, more attention to and acceptance of members of this community and their parents has been requested. They are all children of God and must be welcomed with open arms. This does not mean the Church is in favor of same-sex marriage: we do not have the power to change the sacraments created by the Lord.

Marriage is one of the seven sacraments and provides only for the union of a man and a woman. Leave well enough alone.

Even while I was archbishop of Buenos Aires, I supported and forcefully defended the value of marriage, and today I still want to emphasize, as I did in the apostolic exhortation *Amoris laetitia* (The Joy of Love), that "as for proposals to place unions between homosexual persons on the same level as marriage, there are absolutely no grounds for considering homosexual unions to be in any way similar or even remotely analogous to God's plan for marriage and family," and it is unacceptable "that local churches should be subjected to pressure in this matter and that international bodies should make financial aid to poor countries dependent on the introduction of laws to establish 'marriage' between persons of the same sex."

Civil unions are another matter, and on this subject I have said on many occasions that it is right that these people who experience the gift of love should have the same legal protections as everyone else. Jesus often met and spent time with people who lived on the margins of society, who lived in the existential peripheries, and that is what the Church should be doing today with members of the LGBTQ+ community, who are often marginalized within the Church: make them feel at home, especially those who have been baptized and are in every respect among God's people. And those who have not been baptized and would like to be, or who would like to be godfathers or godmothers: let them be welcomed, please; let them follow a careful pathway to personal discernment.

It is important, however, not to scandalize and disorient the faithful. Bishops and parish priests will have the wisdom to consider these matters case by case. We must walk with these brothers and sisters along the path of faith, just as the Synod on the Family asked, strongly condemning discrimination and acts of violence committed against them. Far too often, they are victims of bullying and acts of sheer cruelty. This is another reason why they cannot and must not be excluded, especially by the Church, which unfortunately has often unfairly considered them to be rotten apples.

I believe it is essential today that we abandon the rigidity of the past, and distance ourselves from a Church that points the finger in condemnation. This is what I meant when I wrote to Cardinal Víctor Manuel Fernández, the prefect of the Dicastery for the Doctrine of the Faith, on the day of his appointment. These attitudes have driven the faithful away. It is therefore important to preserve and promote the faith by placing ourselves close to the people, leaving our embroidery, frills, and lace cuffs in the closet and concentrating instead on the Christian message of compassion and closeness.

A few weeks have passed since that conversation. Life in St. Martha's House carries on as usual, following the strict routines of what is essentially a hotel that also houses a special guest. It is Tuesday morning, the day on which the pope normally has no public engagements or private audiences in the Apostolic Palace. He has gotten down to work early, with the stereo on for some background music—a selection of hits by Azucena Maizani, a singer and composer of Argentine tangos to whom the then-Father Bergoglio, her neighbor in Buenos Aires at the time, gave the last rites in 1970.

The pontiff is at his desk, reading some documents given to him by his secretary yesterday afternoon. He makes notes, marks a few corrections, and annotates a few passages for insertion. It is eight o'clock, and at eight thirty he is expecting a visit from an archbishop friend with whom he is to work on some theological texts. Later he will see his confessor, and other people with whom he has arranged meetings—it is all written down in the personal diary on his desk. He has another half-hour to review the pages he is working on and make a few phone calls.

Also on his desk are the breviary that never leaves his side, more files, and some letters. There is one from Anna in San Donato Milanese, a town near Milan, who is the sole caregiver for her autistic son, Nicolas, now that her husband has left her. Nicolas dreams of talking to the pope. There is one from a seriously ill little boy in Brooklyn, New York, who asks the pope to say a few short prayers for him, and another from a German seminarian, Ludwig, who writes to ask for spiritual support a few weeks before his ordination as a priest.

Francis reads the letter from the young priest-to-be carefully, and in his mind he goes back to 1969, when his own ordination was close and he wrote on a piece of paper the personal profession of faith he often takes out of the drawer when he needs to rediscover that spirit and renew his promise:

I want to believe in God the Father, who loves me like a son, and the Lord Jesus, who has infused my life with His spirit in order to make me smile and thus carry me to the kingdom of eternal life. I believe in my story, which was pierced by the loving gaze of God and, on Spring Day, September 21, led me to an encounter in which He invited me to follow Him. I believe in my pain, made sterile by selfishness, in which I take refuge. I believe in the pettiness of my soul, which seeks to swallow up without giving . . . without giving. I believe other people are good, and that I must love them without fear, never betraying them to obtain safety for myself. I believe in the religious life. I believe I very much want to love. I believe in everyday death, scorching, from which I flee, but which smiles at me and invites me to accept it. I believe in the patience of God, welcoming, kind as a summer night. I believe my dad is in heaven with the Lord. I believe Father Duarte is there too, interceding for my priesthood. I believe in Mary, my mother, who loves me and will never leave me alone. And I expect the surprise of every day in which love, strength, betrayal, and sin will manifest themselves, which will accompany me until my final encounter with that wonderful face whose likeness I do not know, from which I flee constantly, but which I want to know and love. Amen.

Having put away this time-yellowed piece of paper, he picks up the telephone and dials the number of Anna, the mother near Milan who has written to him; he wants to say hello to Nicolas and surprise him. Then he calls the visitor he met a few weeks earlier who had asked how he imagined the Church of the future. This person has emailed some ten pages for the pope to review, a summary of that most recent audience. With the pope's permission, it will be made public, along with summaries of the other audiences he has had.

"Is there hope for humanity, Your Holiness?" the man asks after a short conversation. And the pope answers, while in the background the persuasive voice of the Argentine tango singer, the tanguera, *fills the small gaps in the conversation.*

That question made me think of the times we are living through right now, and I realized that there will be either peace or death in this world—there is no other way. In Europe we have been at war for more than a hundred years, since 1914, and the factories continue to churn out weapons without pause, even now as the world is being devastated by a dispersed Third World War.

I have not so far spoken in depth about the wars in Ukraine or the Middle East here, because there are many initiatives on the table at present and things are in a state of development, but every day my thoughts have gone out, and continue to go out, to those tormented populaces. My heart is in pieces in the face of such horror; I have begged the Lord for the gift of peace. I have said and written much about these wars elsewhere, and I have no tears left. I have seen pictures, heard stories, met witnesses of these tragedies. I have wept for girls and boys who have been snatched away from their families by bombs or who have been orphaned, orphans of war. Such pain, such suffering! And for what? All in the interests of imperialism or out of murderous cynicism. It's scandalous!

As far as Ukraine is concerned, I made myself available immediately, and from the beginning of the war I repeated that I was willing to do anything that might make the guns fall silent. The same applies to the Middle East: I have spoken on the telephone with various international leaders who could make a difference with their actions, reminding everyone of the importance of human life, whether Christian, Muslim, or Jewish. Without distinction of any kind. How are civilian populations to blame? Why must they pay such a high price, even death?

The Holy See has launched a number of diplomatic and humanitarian initiatives, and we hope they will have the desired effects. But we must all, throughout the world, commit ourselves to ensuring that dialogue always prevails, and that those who are responsible understand that bombs do not solve problems but only create new ones. We felt the closeness of the war in Ukraine because it broke out in Europe, but we must not forget that the whole world is suffering the scourge of conflict—in Yemen, Syria, the Democratic Republic of the Congo, South Sudan, Ethiopia, and Myanmar, to give just a few examples.

In many corners of the planet people are suffering from hunger, but paradoxically, rather than thinking about how to resolve that problem, leaders in many countries continue to buy new weapons and develop new technologies for war. There are countries that invest in that sector and base their economies on the deadly trade in weapons. We in the Vatican do not, of course, but since the Holy See is historically involved in financial investments, we know that the most profitable shares are shares in arms manufacturing and abortion drugs. It's scandalous!

The future of the humanity God created depends on the choices we will make: let human beings go back to embracing one another; let them go back to talking about peace, sitting around a table in dialogue, or else it really will be the end. I have hope in human beings, hope that people can learn from their mistakes, improve, and pass on good feelings to future generations.

The work of self-criticism must be done within the Church, too, so that we can take steps that no longer injure the weak and vulnerable. I am reminded of the matter of sexual abuse: How many people have suffered, even to the point of suicide, because of monks or priests who abused them as children? We must think of the victims, listen to them, support them, reminding ourselves that they have been stabbed in the back by those who should have protected them and led them along the path indicated by God. Once again, I would like to ask forgiveness for the sins and grave crimes committed by the Church against these sons and daughters, and ask the Lord to be merciful, for what has happened to these innocent young people is truly satanic and can have no justification.

I think of the cases of sexual abuse uncovered in the United States, in South America, in Eastern Europe, in Ireland; or in Malta, Spain, and Germany, as well as in Italy. The Church must fight this plague with all its strength, and I think the Pontifical Commission for the Protection of Minors that we have established in the Vatican, as well as the offices created in the various dioceses of the world by their episcopal conferences, will be able to contribute to making a difference in the fight against these crimes—receiving allegations, and denouncing both abusers, whether religious or lay, and those who cover up abuse. Today, unlike in the past, when a suitable law was lacking, there are no privileges any more: in cases of abuse, those found guilty in a court of law must serve their sentences with no special protection. Enough of horrors within the Church! We say enough of this wickedness, which besmirches the name of Jesus Christ!

Earlier, I was talking about the future of humanity and how it concerns the Church. But in recent years some people, especially after Benedict XVI's historic resignation, have wondered about the future of the pope. So far, thanks be to God, I have never had reason to think about resigning, because that is an option to be considered, from my point of view, only in the case of serious health problems. I mean it: I have never thought about it because, as I had cause to say some years ago to some African fellow Jesuits, I believe the pope's ministry is *ad vitam*, for life, and I therefore see no justification for giving it up.

Things would change if a serious physical impediment were to arise, and to allow for that case I signed a letter of resignation at the beginning of my papacy, as have other pontiffs, that is deposited with the Vatican Secretariat. If that were to happen, I would not have myself named pope emeritus but simply bishop of Rome emeritus, and I would move to the Basilica of Santa Maria Maggiore to serve as confessor and give communion to the sick.

But this is, I repeat, a distant possibility, because I truly do not have any cause serious enough to make me think of resigning. Some people may have hoped that sooner or later, perhaps after a stay in the hospital, I might make an announcement of that kind, but there is no risk of it: thanks be to God, I enjoy good health, and as I have said, there are many projects to bring to fruition, God willing.

And now we have reached the moment of goodbyes, the end of this book, a journey through history entitled *Life*. Our life: mine; yours, you who are still reading; humanity's. The life that God has given us, which we have built in small steps, making choices, achieving goals, and making mistakes, sometimes serious ones, that have caused us pain and suffering. But in this context the most important lesson must never be forgotten: rereading the story of our own lives is important as a way to remember, and to be able to pass something on to anyone listening.

To learn to live, however, we must all of us learn to love. Let us not forget this! It is the most important lesson we can learn—to love, because love conquers all. By loving we can pull down barriers, we can win battles, we can defeat indifference and hate, we can melt and transform our hearts, throwing our neighbors off balance as Jesus did, who sacrificed Himself on the cross for us sinners and asked nothing in return. A disinterested love that can change the world, that can change the course of history. How many things would have gone differently in the past eighty years of history if love and prayer had motivated human beings, rather than the thirst for power. And speaking of prayer, remember that the world needs it more and more. Let us pray more!

But I ask this of you: please don't forget to pray for me! For, not against!

WORKS CITED

INTRODUCTION

Pope Francis, *Message for the 54th World Communications Day*, January 24, 2020; Copyright © Dicastery for Communication—Libreria Editrice Vaticana

Pope Francis, *General Audience*, October 19, 2022; Copyright © Dicastery for Communication—Libreria Editrice Vaticana

Pope Francis, *General Audience*, August 31, 2022; Copyright © Dicastery for Communication—Libreria Editrice Vaticana

CHAPTER II: The Extermination of the Jews

Pope Francis, *Speech on the occasion of the visit to Yad Vashem Memorial*, May 26, 2014; Copyright © Dicastery for Communication—Libreria Editrice Vaticana

CHAPTER III: Atom Bombs and the End of the War

Pope Pius XII, *Radio message to heads of state and peoples of the world*, August 24, 1939; Copyright © Dicastery for Communication—Libreria Editrice Vaticana

CHAPTER IV: The Cold War and McCarthyism
Pope John XXIII, *Encyclical Letter* Pacem in Terris, *no. 60*, April 11, 1963; Copyright © Dicastery for Communication—Libreria Editrice Vaticana

St. Bede the Venerable, Hom 21; CCL 122, 149–151

CHAPTER V: Landing on the Moon
Pope Paul VI, *Message to the astronauts Neil Armstrong, Edwin Aldrin and Michael Collins on the occasion of the lunar landing*, July 21, 1969; Copyright © Dicastery for Communication—Libreria Editrice Vaticana

CHAPTER VIII: The Fall of the Berlin Wall
Pope John Paul II, *Letter to the Episcopal Conference at Berlin*, November 13, 1989; Copyright © 1989 Dicastery for Communication—Libreria Editrice Vaticana

CHAPTER IX: The Birth of the European Union
Queen Elizabeth II, *address to European Parliament*, May 12, 1992, https://my-european-history.ep.eu/resources/static/images/1493045566884_PE3PE3_AP_DE!1992_DE19920512-110010EN_09941472.pdf

CHAPTER X: The Terrorist Attacks on September 11
Pope John Paul II, *General Audience, September 12, 2001: Prayer of the faithful*; Copyright © Dicastery for Communication—Libreria Editrice Vaticana

CHAPTER XI: The Great Economic Crisis

CHAPTER XII: The Resignation of Benedict XVI

CHAPTER XIII: The COVID-19 Pandemic

Pope Francis, *Extraordinary moment of prayer in a time of epidemic*, March 27, 2020; Copyright © Dicastery for Communication—Libreria Editrice Vaticana

CHAPTER XIV: A History Yet to Be Written

Pope Francis, *Post-Synodal Apostolic Exhortation* Amoris Laetitia, *no. 251*, March 19, 2016; Copyright © Dicastery for Communication—Libreria Editrice Vaticana

ABOUT THE AUTHORS

JORGE MARIO BERGOGLIO was born in Buenos Aires, Argentina, on December 17, 1936, the son of Italian immigrants. Ordained as a Jesuit priest in 1969, he was appointed auxiliary bishop in 1992 and became archbishop of Buenos Aires in 1998. In 2001 he was made a cardinal, and in March 2013 he was elected the 266th supreme pontiff of the Roman Catholic Church, with the papal name of Francis.

FABIO MARCHESE RAGONA is Vaticanist for the Italian Mediaset media group. He reports on the pope for the news programs *Tg5*, *Tg4*, and *Studio Aperto*, and also on TgCom24, an all-news channel for which he produces and presents *Stanze Vaticane* (Vatican Rooms) every Sunday. In January 2021, in a world exclusive, he interviewed Pope Francis in a *Tg5* special watched by 5.5 million people.

ABOUT THE TRANSLATOR

AUBREY BOTSFORD studied modern and medieval languages at the University of Cambridge and worked for many years as an international civil servant and literary translator. His previous translations include novels by Mechtild Borrmann, Katia Fox, Yasmina Khadra, and Enrico Remmert.